EARLY CHILDHOOD ENVIRONMENT RATING SCALE

Updated with additional notes and a new expanded scoresheet

REVISED EDITION

THELMA HARMS
*Director,
Curriculum Development*

RICHARD M. CLIFFORD
*Senior
Investigator*

DEBBY CRYER
*Investigator;
Director, Child Care Program*

*Frank Porter Graham Child Development Institute
The University of North Carolina at Chapel Hill*

TEACHERS
COLLEGE
PRESS

Teachers College, Columbia University
New York and London

Published by Teachers College Press, 1234 Amsterdam Avenue, New York, NY 10027

Cover design by Turner McCollum

ISBN-13 978-0-8077-4549-6
ISBN-10 0-8077-4549-9

Printed on acid-free paper

Manufactured in the United States of America

12   11   8   7

Contents

Preface to the Updated Edition

This updated edition of the ECERS-R is not a revision. It contains the ECERS-Revised Edition with all items and indicators intact. It also includes two helpful additions:

- The widely used Additional Notes available on our website
- A new Expanded Scoresheet, which incorporates a convenient worksheet

This updated edition was produced in response to requests from many scale users who faithfully pasted the Additional Notes into their scales because they found them helpful in establishing and maintaining their accuracy in using the ECERS-R. The new Expanded Scoresheet, which we have used in various states in our own training sessions, has also proved very helpful to both experienced and novice assessors. We believe that both of these additions to the ECERS-R will be helpful.

We are grateful to Cathy Riley for her work in developing the Expanded Scoresheet, and to Elisa Allen, who so ably incorporated the additional materials into this updated edition. As always, feedback from our staff of expert assessors, Cathy Riley, Lisa Waller, Kris Lee, and Tracy Link, has been extremely helpful.

For additional explanations of the meaning of ECERS-R requirements see *All About the ECERS-R* (2003), D. Cryer, T. Harms, C. Riley. Lewisville, NC: Pact House Publishing, ISBN 0-88076-610-7.

Acknowledgments

Our work has been immeasurably enriched by the many colleagues who have used the Early Childhood Environment Rating Scale (ECERS) and generously shared their insights and information with us. Although it is impossible to mention each one who contributed ideas during the years the ECERS has been in use, we want to express our gratitude first to each of the many people who have given us feedback, both informally and formally. This includes colleagues in the United States, Canada, Europe, and Asia whose work in research and program improvement with the ECERS has added greatly to our understanding of quality. Special thanks to the many individuals who responded to our ECERS revision questionnaire.

We want to recognize in particular:

- Participants in our focus groups in Chapel Hill. The focus group on inclusion consisted of Pat Wesley, Ginny Kinney, Kathy Clayton, Sharon Palsha, Deanna Shepherd-Woody, Carla Fenson, Sandy Steele, and Brenda Dennis. The focus group on diversity consisted of Muriel Lundgren, Salma Haidermotha, Valerie Jarvis, Lynette Darkes, Patricia Rodriguez, and Jana Fleming
- Anne Mitchell, Laura Sakai, and Alice Burton, evaluation team members for the Model Centers Initiative in San Francisco, California, who conducted a focus group on diversity with directors and staff, and field tested the ECERS-R in a number of diverse centers
- Research team members from the National Child Care Staffing Study and from the Cost, Quality, and Outcomes Study for sharing their ECERS data with us

- Donna Bryant, Kelly Maxwell, and Ellen Peisner-Feinberg, our colleagues at the Frank Porter Graham Child Development Center, UNC at Chapel Hill, who shared with us data from their studies as well as their valuable experience with the scale
- Adele Richardson Ray, who conducted the extensive literature review and content analysis
- Eva Higgins, who conducted the field tests of the ECERS-R with the assistance of field testers: Nicole Lamb Ives, Canby Robinson, Marianne Mount, Gisele Crawford, Terry Hammersly, Amy Rogers, Cathy Festa, Eleanor Levinson, Noreen Yazejian, and Katherine Polk
- Steve Magers and Dave Gardner, who analyzed the field test data under the direction of Peg Burchinal
- Cathy Riley, who prepared the manuscript and carefully ushered it through endless revisions while somehow maintaining her patience
- Turner McCollum, for his innovative cover design
- Susan Liddicoat, our editor at Teachers College Press, for her patience, interest, and determination to help us make this the best possible scale
- The directors, classroom staff, and children in the 45 classrooms in 35 different centers who graciously permitted us to field test the ECERS-R

We want to thank the A. L. Mailman Family Foundation, the Smith Richardson Foundation, and the Frank Porter Graham Child Development Center Small Grants Program for partially supporting the ECERS revision, and especially for their faith in us and in the value of our work.

Thelma Harms, Richard M. Clifford, and Debby Cryer
Frank Porter Graham Child Development Institute
December, 1997

Introduction to the ECERS-R

The revision of the ECERS has been a long and exacting process. In the revision, our intent was to balance continuity and innovation. On the one hand, we wanted to be sure to retain those features that had, for over 15 years, made the ECERS a useful instrument for both research and program improvement. On the other hand, we wanted to update and expand the instrument to reflect changes in the early childhood field that had occurred since the ECERS was published in 1980, and to incorporate the advances in our own understanding of how to measure quality. During this time, inclusion of children with disabilities and sensitivity to cultural diversity had become important issues in the assessment of program quality. The measurement of quality itself received greater attention through the development of the Accreditation Program of the National Association for the Education of Young Children (NAEYC, 1984) and the publication of several early childhood assessment instruments. During this period of self-examination in the field, the definition of program quality embodied in NAEYC's *Developmentally Appropriate Practice* (Bredekamp, 1986) was revised in 1997 to include a greater emphasis on cultural diversity, family concerns, and individual children's needs (Bredekamp & Copple, 1997).

Our own understanding of how to measure quality was increased through the development of three additional scales using the ECERS format, each with its own improvements and refinements: *Family Day Care Rating Scale* (FDCRS; Harms & Clifford, 1989), *Infant/Toddler Environment Rating Scale* (ITERS; Harms, Cryer, & Clifford, 1990), *School-Age Care Environment Rating Scale* (SACERS; Harms, Jacobs, & White, 1996). Numerous research projects in the United States and abroad had used the ECERS to assess global quality and had discovered significant relationships between ECERS scores and child outcome measures, and between ECERS scores and teacher characteristics, teacher behaviors, and compensation. Along with these research findings, feedback from a number of researchers concerning difficulties with particular items was a valuable resource for the revision. The ECERS was also translated into a number of languages, including Italian, Swedish, German, Portuguese, Spanish, and Icelandic, and was used in an international study (Tietze, Cryer, Bairrão, Palacios, & Wetzel, 1996). Although the basic scale remained the same in the translations, some changes were required in a few of the indicators, and especially in the examples for indicators, to make the various translations culturally relevant. These changes were helpful to us as we undertook our own revision.

In addition, the ECERS was used in a number of ways as a program improvement tool in many different settings, including those serving culturally diverse populations and in inclusive programs. In the 17 years that the ECERS had been used in research and program improvement, a body of evidence of the validity and usefulness of the scale was amassed, but clearly a thorough revision was needed.

Process of Revision

Three main sources of information were used during the process of revision: (1) a content analysis of the relationship of the ECERS to other global quality assessment instruments and documents examining early childhood programmatic issues; (2) data from studies using the ECERS in preschool, child care, and kindergarten settings; and (3) feedback from ECERS users. The content analysis helped to identify additions and deletions to consider; the data from numerous studies using the ECERS gave us information about the range of scores on various items and the relative difficulty of items, as well as their validity. By far the most valuable contribution to the revision came from the feedback provided by researchers and practitioners who had used the ECERS in a variety of ways.

To collect information from ECERS users, three focus groups were held: one to explore how the ECERS functioned in inclusive settings, and two to examine its use in culturally diverse settings. We were fortunate to have access to experts in these two fields who had used the ECERS extensively across the country and could provide specific suggestions. We also held feedback sessions with researchers who had used the ECERS in their studies and who could make suggestions about the content and format from the point of view of research needs. In addition, a questionnaire was circulated to the many individuals, programs, and projects that were known to have used the ECERS extensively, and we received helpful suggestions from people in the United States, Canada, and Europe.

Changes in the ECERS-R

The ECERS-R is indeed a revision of the ECERS; it is not a new scale. The same general rationale and underlying constructs are evident in this revision. The ECERS-R retains the original scale's broad definition of environment, including those spatial, programmatic, and interpersonal features that directly affect the children and adults in an early childhood setting. The seven subscales of the ECERS-R are: Space and Furnishings, Personal Care Routines, Language-Reasoning, Activities, Interaction, Program Structure, and Parents and Staff.

While the subscales in the ECERS-R are not identical with those in the ECERS, the comprehensive definition of environment is apparent. The revision also retains the same format, with each item expressed as a 7-point scale with descriptors for 1 (inadequate), 3 (minimal), 5 (good), and 7 (excellent). The conceptual framework for evaluating quality in the ECERS-R is also consistent with the original ECERS. Levels of program quality are based on current definitions of best practice and on research relating practice to child outcomes. The focus is on the needs of children and how to meet those needs to the best of our current understanding.

While retaining the basic similarities that provide continuity between the ECERS-R and the ECERS, the following changes were made in the revision:

1. The infant-toddler alternate items were omitted; use the *Infant/Toddler Environment Rating Scale* (Harms, Clifford, & Cryer, 1990).
2. The descriptions under quality levels 1, 3, 5, and 7 were written as separate indicators instead of in paragraph form. This follows the pattern set in our other scales, the FDCRS, ITERS, and SACERS.
3. The Notes for Clarification were expanded in order to explain the intent of indicators and to give additional specific information for more accurate scoring.
4. Some items were combined to eliminate redundancy (i.e., ECERS Items 6 and 7 under Furnishings and Display now make up ECERS-R Item 2).
5. Some items were separated into several items to deepen content (i.e., ECERS Item 32 Tone now is separated into ECERS-R Items 31 Discipline and 32 Staff-child interactions).
6. Items were added for areas not covered in the ECERS, such as: health and safety practices; nature/science activities; math/number activities; use of TV, video, and/or computer; interaction items including interactions among children; and several items focusing on staff needs.
7. Indicators and examples were added to many items to make them more inclusive and culturally sensitive. In keeping with the suggestions of our focus groups on inclusion and cultural diversity, we did not develop separate items but rather incorporated indicators and examples throughout the scale.
8. The scoring system was made consistent with that used for the FDCRS, ITERS, and SACERS. In addition, it is possible in the ECERS-R to mark a Yes, No, or, on some items, NA (Not Applicable) for each indicator separately. This will help to identify more clearly the basis for the item quality score.
9. The Notes for Clarification are printed below the item for ease in use.
10. Sample questions are provided below the Notes for Clarification for indicators that are not easily observable.

Our goals for revising the ECERS were to update the content, make the format and scoring instructions more compatible with our other scales, and add indicator scores to permit greater specificity when determining the reason for the item quality score. We believe the ECERS-R has met these goals.

Reliability and Validity

As stated previously, this current version of the ECERS is a revision of the well-known and established original scale. It maintains the same conceptual framework as well as the same basic scoring approach and administration. Since the original version has a long history of research demonstrating that quality as measured by the ECERS has good predictive validity (i.e., Peisner-Feinberg & Burchinal, 1997; Whitebook, Howes, & Phillips, 1990), the revised version would be expected to maintain that form of validity. The major question to be answered here is whether the changes to the scale have affected the interrater reliability.

An extensive set of field tests of the ECERS-R was conducted in the spring and summer of 1997 in 45 classrooms. The authors were not satisfied with the interrater reliabilities obtained and decided that further revision was needed. Data from this first study were used to determine changes needed to obtain a fully reliable instrument. Substantial revisions were made to the first field-test draft of the scale, using the indicator-level reliabilities as a guide to focus the revision process. After the revisions were made, a second test, focusing on interrater reliability, was conducted in a sample of 21 classrooms, equally distributed among high-, medium-, and low-scoring rooms in the initial test. Even though this test was conservative, with minimal chances to develop reliability through the discussions that customarily take place following a practice observation, the results of the second test were quite satisfactory.

Overall, the ECERS-R is reliable at the indicator and item level, and at the level of the total score. The percentage of agreement across the full 470 indicators in the scale is 86.1%, with no item having an indicator agreement level below 70%. At the item level, the proportion of agreement was 48% for exact agreement and 71% for agreement within one point.

For the entire scale, the correlations between the two observers were .921 product moment correlation (Pearson) and .865 rank order (Spearman). The interclass correlation was .915. These figures are all within the generally accepted range with the total levels of agreement being quite high. These overall figures are comparable with the levels of agreement in the original ECERS.

We also examined the internal consistency of the scale at the subscale and total score levels. Subscale internal consistencies range from .71 to .88 with a total scale internal consistency of .92. Table 1 presents the internal consistencies for the seven subscales. These levels of internal consistency indicate that the subscales and total scale can be considered to form reasonable levels of internal agreement providing support for them as separate constructs. Many questions regarding reliability and validity remain unanswered. For example, studies will be required to answer questions such as: To what degree does the revised version maintain the same magnitude of score as the original version? and Do the two versions both predict child development outcomes similarly? In addition, larger data sets will be required to examine empirically the factor structure of the scale. Research on the original ECERS usually has provided two factors, one focusing on the teaching aspect of environments and one on the provision of opportunities aspect (Rossbach, Clifford, & Harms, 1991; Whitebook, Howes, & Phillips, 1990). Further research will be needed to determine the extent to which the ECERS-R reveals the same empirical dimensions.

In summary, the field tests revealed quite acceptable levels of interrater agreement at the three levels of scoring-indicators, items, and total score. In addition, there is support for using the scores of the subscales and the total score to represent meaningful aspects of the environment.

Table 1. Intra-Class Correlations for ECERS-R Subscales

Scale	Interrater Internal Consistency
Space and Furnishings	0.76
Personal Care Routines	0.72
Language-Reasoning	0.83
Activities	0.88
Interaction	0.86
Program Structure	0.77
Parents and Staff	0.71
Total	0.92

References

Bredekamp, S. (Ed.). (1987). *Developmentally appropriate practice in early childhood programs from birth through age 8.* Washington, DC: National Association for the Education of Young Children.

Bredekamp, S., & Copple, C. (Eds.), (1977). *Developmentally appropriate practice in early childhood programs.* Washington, DC: National Association for the Education of Young Children.

Cryer, D., Harms, T., & Riley, C. (2003). *All about the ECERS-R.* Lewisville, NC: Pact House Publishing.

Harms, T., & Clifford, R. M. (1989). *Family Day Care Rating Scale.* New York: Teachers College Press.

Harms, T., Cryer, D., & Clifford, R. M. (1990). *Infant/Toddler Environment Rating Scale.* New York: Teachers College Press.

Harms, T., Jacobs, E., & White, D. (1996). *School-Age Care Environment Rating Scale.* New York: Teachers College Press.

National Association for the Education of Young Children (1984). *Accreditation criteria and procedures of the national academy of early childhood programs.* Washington, DC: Author.

Peisner-Feinberg, E., & Burchinal, M. (1997). Relations between preschool children's child care experiences and concurrent development: The Cost, Quality and Outcomes Study. *Merrill-Palmer Quarterly, 43*(3), 451–477.

Rossbach, H. G., Clifford, R. M., & Harms, T. (1991, April). *Dimensions of learning environments: Cross-national validation of the Early Childhood Environment Rating Scale.* Paper presented at the annual meeting of the American Educational Research Association, Chicago.

Tietze, W., Cryer, D., Bairrão, J., Palacios, J., & Wetzel, G. (1996). Comparisons of observed process quality in early child care and education in five countries. *Early Childhood Research Quarterly, 11*(4), 447–475.

Whitebook, M., Howes, C., & Phillips, D. (1990). *Who cares? Child care teachers and the quality of care in America.* Final report of the National Child Care Staffing Study. Oakland, CA: Child Care Employee Project.

Instructions for Using the ECERS-R

It is important to be accurate in using the ECERS-R—whether you use the scale in your own classroom for self-assessment or as an outside observer for program monitoring, program evaluation, program improvement, or research. A video training package for the ECERS-R is available from Teachers College Press for use in self-instruction or as part of group training. It is preferable to participate in a training sequence led by an experienced ECERS-R trainer before using the scale formally. The training sequence for observers who will use the scale for monitoring, evaluation, or research should include at least two practice classroom observations with a small group of observers, followed by an interrater reliability comparison. Anyone who plans to use the scale should read the following instructions carefully before attempting to rate a program.

Administration of the Scale

1. The scale is designed to be used with one room or one group at a time, for children 2½ through 5 years of age. A block of at least 3 hours should be set aside for observation and rating if you are an outside observer, that is, anyone who is not a member of the teaching staff, (i.e., program directors, consultants, licensing personnel, and researchers). An observation of more than 3 hours in duration is preferable.
2. Before you begin your observation, complete as much as possible of the identifying information on the top of the first page of the Score Sheet. You may need to ask the teacher for some of the information. By the end of the observation, make sure all the identifying information requested on the first page is complete.
3. Take a few minutes at the beginning of your observation to orient yourself to the classroom.
   - You may want to start with Items 1–6 in Space and Furnishings because they are easy to observe.
   - Some items require observation of events and activities that occur only at specific times of the day (i.e., Items 9–12 in Personal Care Routines, Items 7, 8, and 29 covering gross motor play). Be aware of those items so that you can observe and rate them as they occur.
   - Score items that assess interactions only after you have observed for a sufficient time to get a representative picture (i.e., Items 30–33 in Interactions; 34–37 in Program Structure; 41 in Parents and Staff).
   - Items 19–28 in Activities will require both inspection of materials and observation of use of materials.
4. Be careful not to disrupt the ongoing activities while you are observing.

- Maintain a pleasant but neutral facial expression.
- Do not interact with the children unless you see something dangerous that must be handled immediately.
- Do not talk to or interrupt the staff.

5. You need to arrange a time with the teacher to ask questions about indicators you were not able to observe. The teacher should be free of responsibility for children when he or she is answering questions. Approximately 20 minutes will be required for questions. In order to make best use of the time set aside for asking questions:
   - Use the sample questions provided, whenever applicable.
   - If you have to ask questions about items for which no sample questions have been provided, jot your questions down on the Score Sheet or another sheet of paper before talking with the teacher.
   - Ask only those questions needed to decide whether a higher score is possible.
   - Ask questions on one item at a time and take notes or decide on a score before you move on to the next item.
6. Note that the Score Sheet (beginning on p. 75) provides a convenient way of recording the ratings for indicators, items, subscale, and total scores, as well as your comments. The Profile (p. 87) permits a graphic representation of this information.
   - A fresh copy of the Score Sheet is needed for each observation. Permission is hereby given to photocopy the Score Sheet and Profile only, not the entire scale.
   - Ratings should be recorded on the Score Sheet before leaving the program or immediately afterward. Ratings should not be entrusted to memory for later recording.
   - It is advisable to use a pencil on the Score Sheet during the observation so that changes can be made easily.
   - The final Score Sheet entries should be dark enough to photocopy.

Scoring System

1. Read the entire scale carefully, including the Items, Notes for Clarification, and Questions. In order to be accurate, all ratings have to be based as exactly as possible on the indicators provided in the scale items.
2. The scale should be kept readily available and consulted frequently during the entire observation to make sure that the scores are assigned accurately.
3. Examples that differ from those given in the indicators but seem comparable may be used as a basis for giving credit for an indicator.
4. Scores should be based on the current situation that is observed or reported by staff,

not on future plans. In the absence of observable information on which to base your rating, you may use answers given by the staff during the question period to assign scores.

5. When scoring an item, always start reading from 1 (inadequate) and progress upward till the correct score is reached.

6. Ratings are to be assigned in the following way:
   - A rating of 1 must be given if *any* indicator under 1 is scored Yes.
   - A rating of 2 is given when all indicators under 1 are scored No and at least half of the indicators under 3 are scored Yes.
   - A rating of 3 is given when all indicators under 1 are scored No and all indicators under 3 are scored Yes.
   - A rating of 4 is given when all indicators under 3 are met and at least half of the indicators under 5 are scored Yes.
   - A rating of 5 is given when all indicators under 5 are scored Yes.
   - A rating of 6 is given when all indicators under 5 are met and at least half of the indicators under 7 are scored Yes.
   - A rating of 7 is given when all indicators under 7 are scored Yes.
   - A score of NA (Not Applicable) may only be given for indicators or for entire items when "NA permitted" is shown on the scale and on the Score Sheet. Indicators that are scored NA are not counted when determining the rating for an item, and items scored NA are not counted when calculating subscale and total scale scores.

7. To calculate average subscale scores, sum the scores for each item in the subscale and divide by the number of items scored. The total mean scale score is the sum of all item scores for the entire scale divided by the number of items scored.

Alternate Scoring Option

Since each one of the indicators in the ECERS-R can be given a score, it is possible to continue to score the indicators beyond the quality level score assigned to an item. Using the scoring system described above, indicators are typically scored only until an item quality score is assigned. However, if it is desirable, for purposes of research or program improvement, to gain additional information on areas of strength beyond the quality level score, the observer can continue to score all the indicators.

If the alternate scoring option is selected and all indicators are scored, the required observation time and the questioning time will need to be extended considerably. An observation of approximately 3½–4 hours and a questioning time of approximately 45 minutes will be required to complete all indicators. The additional information may, however, be helpful in making plans for specific improvements and in the interpretation of research findings.

The Score Sheet and the Profile

The Score Sheet provides for both indicator and item scores. The indicator scores are Y (Yes), N (No), and NA (Not Applicable), which is permitted only as noted for selected indicators. The item scores are 1 (Inadequate) through 7 (Excellent), and NA (Not Applicable), which is permitted only as noted for selected items. Care should be taken to mark the correct box under Y, N, or NA for each indicator. The numerical item score should be circled clearly (see sample, p. 74).

The expanded version of the Score Sheet included in this updated edition can be used as both a Worksheet and a Score Sheet. In addition to the larger spaces provided for notes, there are questions, charts, and other aids for keeping track of specific information gathered throughout the observation. For example, the number of child-sized chairs and tables, the number of times handwashing is completed, or examples of various categories of materials can now be conveniently recorded and calculated directly on the Score Sheet. The last page of the Score Sheet provides a chart for calculating the "substantial portion of the day" (see Explanations of Terms Used Throughout the Scale below). It also provides space to copy the written schedule and compare it with the observed schedule to determine whether each of the 11 items requiring "substantial portion of the day" has been met.

The Profile on page 87 permits a graphic representation of the scores for all items and subscales. It can be used to compare areas of strengths and weaknesses, and to select items and subscales to target for improvement. There is also space for the mean subscale scores. The profiles for at least two observations can be plotted side by side to present changes visually (see sample, p. 74).

Explanations of Terms Used Throughout the Scale

1. **Accessible** means children can reach and use materials, furnishings, equipment, and so forth. This does not mean that every child has to have access at all times. For example, access may be limited to a certain number of children in an area or limited to certain times of the day. For materials to be considered "accessible," they must be within view of younger preschoolers (2's and 3's). For older preschoolers (4's and 5's), if materials are stored in closed spaces, they can be considered accessible *only* if it is *observed* that children can freely access and use the materials. Generally, for materials to be counted as accessible to children at the Minimal (3) level, children must be able to reach and use the materials for a period of 1 hour a day in a program of 8 hours or more. The 1 hour can be provided at one time or as a combination of several periods throughout the day. This does not mean that each child must have a full hour to use the materials. However, it is required that children have a reasonable chance to use the materials at some time if they wish. Less time is required for programs operating less than 8 hours a day, with the amount of time calculated propor-

tionally, based on the ratio of 1 hour for programs of 8 hours or more. For example, if a program operated for 6 hours a day, this would be ¾ of a full-day program, so the time required would be ¾ of the 1 hour. Use this chart to determine the approximate amount of time needed in programs operating less than 8 hours. For exceptions to this rule, see Items 7, 8, and 23.

Number of hours in operation	2 hrs	3hrs.	4hrs.	5hrs.	6hrs.	7hrs.
Approximate minutes required for accessibility	15	25	30	40	45	50

2. A "**substantial portion of the day**" means at least one-third of the time the children are in attendance. For example, 1 hour out of a 3-hour program, or 3 hours out of a 9-hour program. In calculating whether materials or activities are accessible for a "substantial portion of the day," be sure to ask the teacher questions that give you a reasonable estimate of what happens and what is accessible during the times not observed. Calculate substantial portion of the day based on what is observed, plus what the teacher says is usually done during the rest of the time. In piecing together accessibility of materials in various classrooms or areas to give credit for substantial portion of the day (e.g., outdoors/indoors), the requirements for materials in 5.1 must be met, unless exceptions are specified in notes on individual items. The last page of the expanded version of the Score Sheet is designed to assist in the calculation of "substantial portion of the day" for the 11 items that include this requirement. Space is provided on this page for recording both the planned and observed schedule of daily events. For further information on calculating the substantial portion of the day see *All About the ECERS-R,* pp. xviii and xix.

3. In order to differentiate the meaning of the words "**some,**" "**many**," and "**varied**," the materials in several items are separated into categories in the Notes for Clarification. For example, gross motor equipment is separated into *stationary equipment* and *portable equipment*; fine motor materials are separated into *small building toys, art materials, manipulatives,* and *puzzles*; nature/science includes categories of materials such as *collections of natural objects, living things, nature/science books, games,* or *toys,* and *nature/science activities* such as cooking and simple experiments. Terms such as "some," "many," or "variety" are used throughout the scale. We have provided numbers to guide decision making for many of these terms. However, the actual number required will depend on the number of children enrolled, and the ages and abilities of those children. In cases where there are small groups of children, the numbers provided are likely to be reasonable. However, in classrooms with 15 or more children, more materials may be needed. In considering the difference between "variety" and "many," think about a meal provided as a buffet, compared with a meal with several courses, but not as much choice. "Variety" of choices will be provided in the buffet, while this is not necessarily true in the meal.

The term "some" occurs most frequently in indicators that represent a Minimal (3) level of quality, although occasionally it occurs at higher levels. In determining how much is needed to give credit for "some" in an indicator, consider the requirements in the parallel indicators at the lower and next higher level of quality. For example, if under Inadequate (1) no materials are required, then "some" would mean "one or more." In cases where a plural is used with the term "some," then more than one would be required to give credit. When terms such as "very few" or "very little" or "rarely" are used under Inadequate, then "some" represents a mid-point between what is required for the 1 and for the 5 quality levels. Specific numbers are given in the notes for particular indicators.

4. "**Staff**" generally refers to the adults who are directly involved with the children—the teaching staff. In the scale, staff is used in the plural because there is usually more than one staff member working with a group. When individual staff members handle things differently, it is necessary to arrive at a score that characterizes the overall impact on the children of all the staff members. For example, in a room where one staff member is very verbal and the other is relatively nonverbal, the score is determined by how well the children's needs for verbal input are being met.

In all items involving any type of interaction, "staff" refers to those adults who are in the classroom and who work with the children daily (or almost daily), for a substantial portion of the day. This can include volunteers, if they are in the classroom for the required amount of time. Adults who are in the classroom for short periods of the day, or who are not a regular daily part of the classroom, do not count in evaluating whether the requirements of the item are met. For example, if a therapist, parent, or the director of a program comes into the classroom and interacts with children, for short or irregular periods, these interactions do not count in scoring the item, *unless the interaction is very negative.* As an exception, in parent co-operatives or lab schools, whose usual staffing pattern includes different people as teaching assistants daily, these assistants should be counted as staff.

5. The term "**weather permitting**" is used in several items of the scale with regard to when children can participate in outdoor activities. "Weather permitting" means *almost every day,* unless there is active precipitation, extremely hot or cold conditions, or public announcements that advise people to remain indoors due to weather conditions such as high levels of pollution and extreme cold or heat that might cause health problems. Children should be dressed properly and taken outdoors on most days. This might require that the schedule be changed to allow children outdoor play in the early morning if it will be very hot later in the day. Or it might require that the program ensure that children have boots and a change of clothes for a day when the grass is wet. After bad weather, staff should check the outdoor area, dry off equipment, sweep away water, or block off puddles, and so forth, as needed before children go out. Programs with protected outdoor areas, such as a deck or patio, are more likely to be able to meet the requirements for allowing outdoor activity daily, weather permitting.

Overview of the Subscales and Items of the ECERS-R

Inadequate		Minimal		Good		Excellent
1	2	3	4	5	6	7

SPACE AND FURNISHINGS

1. Indoor space

1.1 Insufficient space for children, adults, and furnishings. *

1.2 Space lacks adequate lighting, ventilation, temperature control, or sound-absorbing materials. *

1.3 Space in poor repair (Ex. peeling paint on walls and ceiling; rough, damaged floors). *

1.4 Space poorly maintained (Ex. floors left sticky or dirty; trash cans overflowing).

3.1 Sufficient indoor space for children, adults, and furnishings. *

3.2 Adequate lighting, ventilation, temperature control, and sound-absorbing materials. *

3.3 Space in good repair.

3.4 Space reasonably clean and well maintained. *

3.5 Space is accessible to all children and adults currently using the classroom (Ex. ramps and handrails for people with disabilities, access for wheelchairs and walkers). * *NA permitted.*

5.1 Ample indoor space that allows children and adults to move around freely (Ex. furnishings do not limit children's movement; sufficient space for equipment needed by children with disabilities). *

5.2 Good ventilation, some natural lighting through windows or skylight.

5.3 Space is accessible to children and adults with disabilities. *

7.1 Natural light can be controlled (Ex. adjustable blinds or curtains).

7.2 Ventilation can be controlled (Ex. windows can open; ventilating fan used by staff). *

(See Notes for Clarification on next page)

*Notes for Clarification

1.1. Base space needs on largest number of children attending at one time.

1.1, 1.2, 3.1, & 3.2. Base score of this item only on the observed functioning of the space in the room used by the group most of the day. "Insufficient space" means not enough space. Score "yes" only if room is extremely crowded. "Sufficient space" means enough space to function adequately. Do not give credit for 3.1 if adequate space is due to lack of basic furnishings and equipment. If a classroom is terribly noisy, so that conversations are difficult and noise levels are obviously uncomfortable for classroom users, then do not give credit for adequate sound-absorbing materials, even if a number of such materials are present (rugs, ceiling tiles). If noise typically is not at a comfortable level, for whatever reason, the sound absorbing materials are not effective enough. This is true even if the noise is not actually coming from within the classroom being observed.

1.3. "Poor repair" means that there are major repair problems that present health and/or safety risks.

3.4. It is expected that there will be some messiness from the regular activities of the day. "Reasonably clean" means that there is evidence of daily maintenance, such as floors being swept and mopped, and that big messes, such as a juice spill, are cleaned up promptly.

3.5, 5.3. In order for the indoor space to be considered minimally acceptable, it must be accessible to children and adults with disabilities who are currently a part of the program. If no children or adults with disabilities are currently part of the program, score NA for indicator 3.5. However, for a score of 5, accessibility is required regardless of whether or not individuals with disabilities are involved in the program. Therefore only a score of N or Y is allowed for 5.3.

5.1. To assess whether indoor space is "ample," consider the various activity areas as well as routine care areas. For example, look to see if the block or housekeeping area allows plenty of free movement for children to play, as well as for storage and use of the materials and equipment needed in the area. Do not give credit for ample space if at least two activity areas are crowded, even if there is ample space for routines.

5.3. To give credit for this indicator, the classroom and the bathroom (including toilet stalls) must be accessible to individuals with disabilities. Doorways must be 32 inches wide. The door handles must be operable with limited use of hands. The entrance door threshold should be ½" high or less and, if over ¼", must be beveled to make it easier to roll over. However, access to the various play areas in the room is considered under Item 4. Room arrangement for play, and not in this item. Adaptations to toilets (Ex., bars to help with stability) are considered in Item 2, indicators 3.3 & 5.3.

    If there are 2 or more bathrooms used by the children in the classroom, only one of them must be accessible. Accessibility to the building itself, and to the floor where the classroom is located, is also considered under this indicator. The definition of *accessible* should be based on the information in this note, with no additional requirements.

7.2. Doors to outside count as ventilation control only if they can be left open without posing a safety threat (for example, if they have a locking screen door or safety gate to keep children from leaving the room unattended).

Inadequate		Minimal		Good		Excellent
1	2	3	4	5	6	7

2. Furniture for routine care, play, and learning*

1.1 Insufficient basic furniture for routine care, play, and learning (Ex. not enough chairs for all children to use at the same time; very few open shelves for toys). *

1.2 Furniture is generally in such poor repair that children could be injured (Ex. splinters or exposed nails, wobbly legs on chairs).

3.1 Sufficient furniture for routine care, play, and learning.

3.2 Most furniture is sturdy and in good repair. *

3.3 Children with disabilities have the adaptive furniture they need (Ex. adaptive chairs or bolsters are available for children with physical disabilities). *
NA permitted.

5.1 Most furniture is child-sized. *

5.2 All furniture is sturdy and in good repair. *

5.3 Adaptive furniture permits inclusion of children with disabilities with peers (Ex. child using special chair can sit at table with others). *
NA permitted.

7.1 Routine care furniture is convenient to use (Ex. cots/mats stored for easy access). *

7.2 Woodwork bench, sand/water table, or easel used. *

(See Notes for Clarification on next page)

*Notes for Clarification

Item 2. Remember to consider furnishings for play, and not just routine care furnishings, when scoring all indicators in this item. Basic furniture: tables and chairs used for meals/snacks and activities; mats or cots for rest or nap; cubbies or other storage for children's things; low open shelves for play/learning materials. To be given credit for low open shelves, they must be used for toys and materials that children can reach by themselves.

1.1. "Insufficient basic furniture" means *not enough* or an *insufficient number* of pieces of the basic furniture needed for routines, play, and learning listed in the notes for clarification. If most of the toys are stored in crates or toy boxes and there are very few open shelves, a score of "Yes" is appropriate.

3.2. Sturdiness is a property of the furniture itself (i.e., will not break, fall over, or collapse when used). If sturdy furniture is placed so that it can be easily knocked over, this is a problem with safety (see Item 14. Safety practices), not the sturdiness of the furniture.

3.3, 5.3. If there are no children with disabilities enrolled or if children with disabilities do not need adaptive furniture, mark NA for 3.3 and 5.3.

5.1. This indicator only addresses the size of tables and chairs for children. If cubbies or other furnishings present problems due to size, consider this under 7.1.

While seated back in a chair, children's feet should be able to touch the floor (not necessarily rest flat on the floor); children should not have to perch on edge of chair to touch floor. Children also need to be able to rest their elbows on the table and fit their knees comfortably under the table. Rate here also if chairs and/or tables are too small for the children. Check child-sized several times during observation, including when all children are seated together, such as at lunch. If 75% of children are able to use child-sized tables and chairs, give credit for this indicator.

Since children are different sizes at different ages, the intent here is that furniture should be the right size for the children in care. Furniture that is smaller than adult-sized may be the right size for a 6- or 7-year-old, but not small enough for a 2- or 3-year-old.

5.2. Don't be overly perfectionistic when scoring this indicator. If there is only a very minor problem that does not create a likely safety hazard, then give credit. For example, if a chair or table is slightly wobbly, but will not collapse or cause falls, or if a vinyl-covered couch is slightly worn, but foam is not exposed, then do not count off for these small things, unless there are a substantial number of small problems causing an overall impression of poor repair.

7.1. Cubbies for storage of children's possessions must be in the classroom to be considered convenient, because of difficulties with supervision.

7.2. In order to give credit, it is not necessary to see the furnishing being used, but it must be obvious that it is used for the appropriate activity and not, for example, only for storage. If unsure, ask staff how and when furnishing is used.

Inadequate		Minimal		Good		Excellent
1	2	3	4	5	6	7

3. Furnishings for relaxation and comfort*

1.1 No soft furnishings accessible to children (Ex. upholstered furniture, cushions, rugs, bean bag chair). *

1.2 No soft toys accessible to children (Ex. stuffed animals, soft dolls). *

3.1 Some soft furnishings accessible to children (Ex. carpeted play space, cushions). *

3.2 Some soft toys accessible to children. *

5.1 Cozy area accessible to children for a substantial portion of the day. *

5.2 Cozy area is not used for active physical play. *

5.3 Most soft furnishings are clean and in good repair. *

7.1 Soft furnishings in addition to cozy area accessible to children (Ex. cushions in dramatic play area, several rug areas or wall-to-wall carpeting). *

7.2 Many clean, soft toys accessible to children. *

---

*Notes for Clarification

Item 3. "Furnishings for relaxation and comfort" means softness provided for children during learning and play activities. Routine care furnishings such as cots, blankets, and pillows used for naps are not considered when scoring this item.

1.1. See "Explanation of Terms Used Throughout the Scale" on pp. 6–7 for the definition of "accessible."

1.2. Examples of soft toys include cloth puppets (even if they have hard heads or hands), dolls that are completely soft or that have soft bodies, and soft toy animals of all sizes, from those that can be held in one hand to large animals children can sit or lie on.

3.1. "Some soft furnishings" means that there are at least two soft furnishings in the room being observed that the children may use in play.

3.2. "Some soft toys accessible" means at least three soft toys are accessible to children.

5.1. A "cozy area" is a clearly defined space with a substantial amount of softness where children may lounge, daydream, read, or play quietly. For example, it might consist of a soft rug with several cushions, an upholstered couch, or a covered mattress with cushions. The cozy area must provide a substantial amount of softness for the children. This means that the cozy furnishings must allow a child to completely escape the normal hardness of the typical early childhood classroom. One *small* thing, in itself, does not create a cozy area. For example, a small padded chair, small child-sized beanbag chair, a few small stuffed animals, or a carpeted corner, are each not enough by themselves. However, credit could be given for a combination of such furnishings. Credit might be given for large furnishings, such as a mattress, couch, or adult-sized bean bag chair, if they provide the required substantial amount of softness.

   See "Explanation of Terms Used Throughout the Scale" on p. 7 for the definition of "a substantial portion of the day."

5.1, 5.2. If there are two or more cozy areas, each area does not need to meet the requirements of 5.1 and 5.2. However, there must always be one area, providing a substantial amount of softness where children can depend on being able to relax, that is *not* used for active physical play. It must be obvious that a child who wants to use a cozy area will not be constantly interrupted by children involved in active play. A combination of all areas can be used to judge whether a cozy area is accessible for a substantial portion of the day.

5.2. The cozy area may be used for short periods as a group space (e.g., for dancing or circle time), but it should be protected from active play for most of the day. It should be away from active play equipment and have protection from active children (through placement or a barrier). It should not be located where there is a lot of traffic. Staff should be diligent to ensure that active children do not interfere with a child in the cozy area by jumping on or running into the child who is relaxing.

5.3. Look especially to see that there are no tears in the covers of beanbag chairs, cushions, and couches that expose the padding or stuffing. "Most soft furnishings" means almost all, with only one or two minor exceptions.

7.1. Give credit only for additional soft furnishings that can be used during play. If there is carpet under tables that cannot be used to sit or play on, credit cannot be given for soft furnishings.

7.2. "Many" means enough soft toys so that children do not have to compete over them: for 2's and 3's at least two soft toys for each child; 4's and K's at least 10 toys or, if more than 20 children are allowed to attend at one time, enough for half the group size allowed.

Inadequate		Minimal		Good		Excellent
1	2	3	4	5	6	7

4. Room arrangement for play

1.1 No interest centers defined. *	3.1 At least two interest centers defined. *	5.1 At least three interest centers defined and conveniently equipped (Ex. water provided near art area; shelving adequate for blocks and manipulatives). *
1.2 Visual supervision of play area is difficult. *	3.2 Visual supervision of play area is not difficult.	5.2 Quiet and active centers placed to not interfere with one another (Ex. reading or listening area separated from blocks or housekeeping). *

7.1 At least five different interest centers provide a variety of learning experiences. *

7.2 Centers are organized for independent use by children (Ex. labeled open shelves; labeled containers for toys; open shelves are not over-crowded; play space near toy storage). *

3.3 Sufficient space for several activities to go on at once (Ex. floor space for blocks, table space for manipulatives, easel for art). *

3.4 Most spaces for play are accessible to children with disabilities enrolled in the group.
NA permitted.

5.3 Space is arranged so most activities are not interrupted (Ex. shelves placed so children walk around, not through, activities; placement of furniture discourages rough play or running).

7.3 Additional materials available to add to or change centers.

*Notes for Clarification

1.1, 3.1, 5.1, 7.1. An interest center is an area where materials, organized by type, are stored so that they are accessible to children, and appropriately furnished play space is provided for children to participate in a particular kind of play. Examples of interest centers are art activities, blocks, dramatic play, reading, nature/science, and manipulatives/fine motor.

1.2. Do not score "Yes" unless area is very difficult to supervise. Take ages of children into consideration when deciding on a score.

3.3. Look to see that there is space enough for at least three different types of activities to go on at the same time for some period of the day.

5.2. Look for a separation in physical space, actual distance between active or noisy centers and the more quiet centers. A barrier, such as open shelves, does not sufficiently cut down on noise. To give credit, *all* quiet areas must be separated from noisy areas.

7.2. To get credit for this indicator, *almost* all materials in all centers must be organized for independent use. Labels are not required in all areas. Other examples that apply are shelves not overcrowded, see-through or labeled containers used to store toys, materials such as puzzles and games easy to take off shelves, sets of materials in bins when needed, and containers with tops easily opened by children.

Question

7.3. Are there any additional materials available that you add to the interest centers?

15

Inadequate		Minimal		Good		Excellent
1	2	3	4	5	6	7

5. Space for privacy*

1.1 Children not allowed to play alone or with a friend, protected from intrusion by other children.

3.1 Children are allowed to find or create space for privacy (Ex. behind furniture or room dividers, in outdoor play equipment, in a quiet corner of the room).

3.2 Space for privacy can be easily supervised by staff. *

5.1 Space set aside for one or two children to play, protected from intrusion by others (Ex. no-interruption rule; small space protected by shelves). *

5.2 Space for privacy accessible for use for a substantial portion of the day. *

7.1 More than one space available for privacy.

7.2 Staff set up activities for one or two children to use in private space, away from general group activities (Ex. two pegboards at a small table in a quiet corner; computer for one or two children to use). *

---

*Notes for Clarification

Item 5. The intent of space for privacy is to give children relief from the pressures of group life. Isolation from the group as a punishment is not given credit under this item. A place where one or two children can play protected from intrusion by other children, yet be supervised by staff, is considered space for privacy. Private space can be created by using physical barriers such as book shelves; by enforcing the rule that children may not interrupt one another; by limiting the number of children working at a table placed in an out-of-traffic area. Examples of space for privacy are a small loft area; activity centers where use is limited to one or two children; a large cardboard box with cut-out windows, door, and a cushion inside; a small outdoor play house. (For a definition of space for privacy see *All About the ECERS-R*, pp. 35, 39, 40.)

3.2. All spaces used for privacy must be easily supervised by staff.

5.1. Staff must enforce the protection rule, if needed, in order to be given credit for this indicator.

5.2. This indicator applies only to the space "set aside" for privacy in 5.1. If credit is not given for 5.1, then credit cannot be given for 5.2.

7.2. "Staff" here refers to the regular teaching staff in the room. Specialists who come into the room specifically to work with one or two children do not count for this indicator. See "Explanation of Terms Used Throughout the Scale" on p. 7 for definition of staff.

Question

7.2. Do you ever set up activities for just one or two children, away from the activities for the rest of the children? If so, please give examples.

Inadequate		Minimal		Good		Excellent
1	2	3	4	5	6	7

6. Child-related display

1.1 No materials displayed for children.

1.2 Inappropriate materials for predominant age group (Ex. materials in preschool class-room designed for older school-aged children or adults; pictures showing violence). *

3.1 Appropriate materials for predominant age group (Ex. photos of children; nursery rhymes; beginning reading and math for older preschoolers and kindergartners; seasonal displays). *

3.2 Some children's work displayed. *

5.1 Much of the display relates closely to current activities and children in group (Ex. artwork or photos about recent activities). *

5.2 Most of the display is work done by the children. *

5.3 Many items displayed on child's eye level.

7.1 Individualized children's work predominates. *

7.2 Three-dimensional child-created work (Ex. playdough, clay, carpentry) displayed as well as flat work. *

---

*Notes for Clarification

1.2. Materials must be meaningful to the children to be considered appropriate. Score "Yes" if over 50% of the display in the room is inappropriate for over 50% of the children *or* if any of the displayed materials show violence or indicate prejudice.

3.1. "Appropriate" means suitable for the developmental level of the age group and the individual abilities of the children. This concept is also referred to as developmentally appropriate and is used in a number of items in the scale. Consider only the display in the room(s) where children spend the majority of the time. Score "Yes" if 75% of display is appropriate for the children, and none is violent or prejudicial.

3.2. "Some" means that at least two pieces of children's work are displayed and can be easily seen by children.

5.1. "Much of the display" means about 30% of the materials displayed. The first part of this indicator requires that a relationship exist between what is displayed and the activities that the current group of children is experiencing. The intent here is for the teacher to use the display for children as a teaching tool that changes as topics of interest change and that adds more information to the children's experiences. For instance, if the group is talking about the season of the year, a science project they are doing, or an upcoming field trip, these things should be represented in the display. Recently completed artwork that does not relate to other things going on in the room does not count for this indicator. If needed, supplement observed information by asking if any of the display relates to topics of interest covered within the last month.

5.1. (cont.) The second part of this indicator requires that the children themselves be represented in the display. Look to see if there are photos of the children in the group on display, or self-portraits, or a height-chart with names. Photos of the children are not required, but the display should relate to the children in the group (e.g., stories dictated by children, charts done with children's input).

5.2. Base score on overall impression of whether children's art is well represented in the display. Consider what you feel when you have looked around the room from various areas. Counting number of pieces of artwork is not necessary. If 50/50, or too close to tell, give credit for most of the display done by children. If a detailed search is needed to find the children's work, then do not give credit.

7.1. Score "Yes" if more than 50% of children's displayed work is individualized. Individualized work means that each child has selected the subject and/or media and has carried out the work in his or her own creative way. Thus, individualized products look quite different from one another. Projects where children follow a teacher's example and little creativity is allowed are not considered individualized work. (See *All About the ECERS-R*, pp. 51, 52, 53 for further definition of individualized.)

7.2. "Three-dimensional" work must have height, width, and depth. The children must be able to build up and out as they make "junk," styrofoam, or wood sculptures, or use clay or play-dough (but not as in using cookie cutters with play-dough). Gluing things to a flat surface (as in gluing material scraps or styrofoam "peanuts" to a flat piece of paper or cardboard) is not counted as 3-D.

Inadequate		Minimal		Good		Excellent
1	2	3	4	5	6	7

7. Space for gross motor play*

1.1 No outdoor or indoor space used for gross motor/physical play.

1.2 Gross motor space is very dangerous (Ex. access requires long walk on busy street; same space used for play and parking lot; unfenced area for preschoolers). *

3.1 Some space outdoors or indoors used for gross motor/physical play. *

3.2 Gross motor space is generally safe. (Ex. sufficient cushioning under climbing equipment; fenced in outdoor area). *

5.1 Adequate space outdoors and some space indoors. *

5.2 Space is easily accessible for children in group (Ex. on same level and near classroom; no barriers for children with disabilities).

5.3 Space is organized so that different types of activities do not interfere with one another (Ex. play with wheel toys separated from climbing equipment and ball play). *

7.1 Outdoor gross motor space has a variety of surfaces permitting different types of play (Ex. sand, black top, wood chips; grass). *

7.2 Outdoor area has some protection from the elements (Ex. shade in summer, sun in winter, wind break, good drainage). *

7.3 Space has convenient features (Ex. close to toilets and drinking water, accessible storage for equipment; class has direct access to outdoors). *

(See Notes for Clarification and Question on next page)

18

*Notes for Clarification

Item 7. In assessing space for gross motor play, include both outdoor and indoor areas, except where only one is specified in an indicator. All areas regularly available and/or used for gross motor activities should be considered in scoring this item, even if children are not observed in the area.

1.2, 3.2. Although no gross motor area that challenges children can ever be completely safe, the intent of this indicator is that major causes of serious injury are minimized, such as injury from falls onto inadequate cushioning surfaces, or entrapment, pinching of body parts, and protrusions from non-gross motor equipment that is in the space. Safety of the equipment is covered in Item 8. Gross motor equipment. Issues related to safety of the space (not the gross motor equipment) is considered in this item. Fall zones, with required cushioning surfaces are considered part of the space (not equipment), and thus considered here. Height and velocity of falls should be considered when determining whether a fall zone with cushioning surface is needed. Anything permitted by the staff to be used for stimulating active play that could lead to a fall with serious consequences must have an adequate fall zone.

Note that the requirements for verifying the resilience of materials not covered in the chart on Playground Information in *All About the ECERS-R* on pp. 62 and 63, such as poured or installed foam or rubber surfaces, is as follows: the child care provider must provide written proof of meeting ASTM 1292 requirements for the material used under equipment.

Although the Consumer Product Safety Commission Guidelines for cushioning surfaces and fall zones apply only to anchored equipment, for purposes of scoring, these standards should be applied to anything used for gross motor play, in which falls onto inadequate cushioning surfaces can occur. (See *All About the ECERS-R*, pp. 57–67 for further information.)

Any *non-gross motor equipment* that is in the space (such as fences, storage sheds, air conditioning units, dramatic play structures, benches, picnic tables, water play areas) must also be assessed in this item, for safety problems they might pose, such as protrusions on low fences, obstructions in a trike path or accessibility to dangerous objects.

3.1. "Some space" means that indoor and/or outdoor space is used for gross motor play by the children in the group for at least 1 hour each day in a program operating 4 or more hours per day. In programs operating less than 4 hours per day, at least ½ hour is required.

3.2. A space can be considered generally safe even if it cannot be easily supervised. The ability to supervise space is not considered in this item, but in Item 29. Supervision of gross motor activities. Consider all spaces used at any time for gross motor play including hallways, covered patios, parking lots, and so forth.

5.1. For a rating of 5, space must be adequate for the size of the group using the area. Find out if class groups rotate or if several groups use the space at the same time. Some indoor space must be available for use for gross motor play, especially in bad weather. This space may usually be used for other activities. Classroom space or hallways can count as "some indoor space," but only if the space is reasonably large and open (through moving furniture, if necessary). In some areas, where the climate is never extreme for long periods and a covered outdoor area can be used year-round, this can also count as some indoor space. When required by environmental conditions (e.g., extreme weather or pollution; dangerous social conditions), facilities may be given credit for this indicator if they have adequate space indoors and some space outdoors.

5.3. To score this indicator, observe to see that the various activities in the gross motor space do not interfere with each other (e.g., that children are not in great danger of tripping over toys as they run across the space, that children coming down a slide will not bump into anything, or that wheel toys do not usually go through areas with other types of play and "run people down.")

7.1. At least one hard and one soft play surface large enough to permit a type of play must be accessible daily outdoors.

7.2. Only one example of protection from the elements must be observed to give credit for 7.2. But the protection observed must match the most prevalent adverse conditions caused by the elements in the local area.

7.3. To give credit for 7.3, at least two convenient features must be observed.

Question

5.1. Is there any indoor space that you use for gross motor play, especially in bad weather?

Inadequate		Minimal		Good		Excellent
1	2	3	4	5	6	7

8. Gross motor equipment*

1.1 Very little gross motor equipment used for play.

1.2 Equipment is generally in poor repair.

1.3 Most of the equipment is not appropriate for the age and ability of the children (Ex. 6-foot tall open slide for preschoolers; adult-sized basketball hoop). *

3.1 Some gross motor equipment accessible to all children for at least one hour daily. *

3.2 Equipment is generally in good repair. *

3.3 Most of the equipment is appropriate for the age and ability of the children. *

5.1 There is enough gross motor equipment so that children have access without a long wait. *

5.2 Equipment stimulates a variety of skills (Ex. balancing, climbing, ball play, steering and pedaling wheel toys). *

5.3 Adaptations made or special equipment provided for children in group with disabilities. *
NA permitted.

7.1 Both stationary and portable gross motor equipment are used. *

7.2 Gross motor equipment stimulates skills on different levels (Ex. tricycles with and without pedals; different sizes of balls; both ramp and ladder access to climbing structure). *

(See Notes for Clarification on next page)

Item 8. "Gross motor equipment" includes *anything* provided for or regularly permitted by the staff to be used for stimulating gross motor activity. This includes manufactured, custom-made, and/or natural objects used for climbing, sliding, balancing, or other gross motor activity. It does not include objects meant to be used for other purposes, such as benches to sit on, shade trees, or shelves children are not supposed to climb, unless children are regularly permitted to use them as gross motor equipment. Categories of gross motor equipment: *stationary equipment* such as swings, slides, climbing equipment, overhead ladders; *portable equipment* such as balls and sports equipment, wheel toys, tumbling mats, jump ropes, bean bags, and ring toss game. When rating gross motor equipment, consider equipment both indoors and outdoors.

1.3, 3.2, 3.3. The safety of gross motor equipment is handled in this item, in terms of appropriateness and condition. Safety of fall zones, with cushioning surfaces, and all other hazards present in the space, are handled in Item 7. Space for gross motor play.

3.1. Programs operating for at least 8 hours a day must have at least 1 hour of access to gross motor equipment daily. Less time is required for programs operating less than 8 hours a day, with the amount of time calculated proportionally, based on the ratio of 1 hour for programs of 8 hours or more. For programs of 4 hours or less, at least half an hour of access is required (see chart provided in "Explanation of Terms Used Throughout the Scale" on p. 7 to determine approximate amount of time required for part-day programs of more than 4 hours).

   "Some" means that all children can have access to equipment, during the gross motor time.

3.3. In a mixed-aged group, appropriate equipment must be available for the different abilities represented. Consider especially the appropriateness of the stationary equipment such as climbers, since they are permanent installations and always accessible. "Most" means 75% of the stationary equipment is suitable for the age and ability of the children being observed.

5.1. "Enough" means that children have interesting options for gross motor play and do not have to wait long periods of time to use the equipment they *choose* to use. Consider both portable and stationary equipment.

5.2. To meet the requirement for a "variety of skills," the equipment children can use should stimulate the development of 7–9 different skills. Generally 1 piece of equipment will not provide this variety, but in the case of a very complex climber the indicator might be true. Other skills, besides those listed in the example, might include pulling/pushing, hanging by arms, swinging, jumping, hopping, using a jump rope, operating a hula hoop, tossing things into containers, catching, throwing, or kicking. Observe to see how many skills the equipment encourages and list them. Consider both portable and stationary equipment.

5.3. Adaptations include physical modifications to existing equipment or specially designed equipment as well as help from staff to enable children with disabilities to have gross motor experiences similar to those of their peers. Score NA if no children requiring adaptations are enrolled in the group being observed.

7.1. "Portable" equipment means that the portability is part of the play potential for children (e.g., wheel toys, balls, jump ropes, hula hoops, roller skates, bats, tennis rackets). Equipment that children cannot or should not move as part of play is considered stationary, even though it may not be anchored, and therefore can be moved.

7.2. Consider ages of children and what challenges them to determine whether equipment stimulates skills on different levels.

Inadequate		Minimal		Good		Excellent
1	2	3	4	5	6	7

PERSONAL CARE ROUTINES

9. Greeting/departing*

1.1 Greeting of children is often neglected. *

1.2 Departure not well organized.

1.3 Parents not allowed to bring children into the classroom.

3.1 Most children greeted warmly (Ex. staff seem pleased to see children, smile, use pleasant tone of voice). *

3.2 Departure well organized (Ex. children's things ready to go).

3.3 Parents allowed to bring children into the classroom.

5.1 Each child is greeted individually (Ex. staff say "hello" and use child's name; use child's primary language spoken at home to say "hello"). *

5.2 Pleasant departure (Ex. children not rushed, hugs and good-byes for everyone).

5.3 Parents greeted warmly by staff. * *NA permitted.*

7.1 When they arrive, children are helped to become involved in activities, if needed.

7.2 Children busily involved until departure (Ex. no long waiting without activity; allowed to come to comfortable stopping point in play).

7.3 Staff use greeting and departure as information sharing time with parents. * *NA permitted.*

(See Notes for Clarification and Question on next page)

Item 9. In case only a few children are observed being greeted (or departing), generalize based on that sample.

1.1. Score "Yes" when children are usually (75% of the time) *not* acknowledged by staff, either verbally or non-verbally, either positively or neutrally, upon entering the classroom, or very soon after their arrival (within 1–2 minutes).

3.1. "Most" requires that at least 75% of the children are greeted warmly, and any new staff member greets the children as well.

5.1. Observe greeting very carefully to see if each child is actually greeted, and that the greeting is personal and positive (e.g., caregiver makes eye contact and smiles, uses child's real name or nickname, says something to child or asks something). (For suggestions on accurately assessing greeting and departing, see *All About the ECERS-R*, pp. 80–85).

5.3. To give credit, each parent does not have to be "greeted warmly" during the observation, but it must be obvious that, in general (approximately 75% of the time), parents are treated in this way.

5.3, 7.3. If children are not brought to the program by their parents, mark NA for 5.3 and 7.3, and rate communication between parents and staff in Item 38. Provisions for parents.

7.3. To give credit, each parent does not have to receive information from the staff at greeting and departing, but it must be observed that in general, parents are treated this way.

Question

Could you describe what happens each day when the children and parents arrive and leave?

Inadequate		Minimal		Good		Excellent
1	2	3	4	5	6	7

10. Meals/snacks

1.1 Meal/snack schedule is inappropriate (Ex. child is made to wait even if hungry).

1.2 Food served is of unacceptable nutritional value. *

1.3 Sanitary conditions not usually maintained (Ex. most children and/or adults do not wash hands before handling food; tables not sanitized; toileting/diapering and food preparation areas not separated). *

1.4 Negative social atmosphere (Ex. staff enforce manners harshly; force child to eat; chaotic atmosphere).

1.5 No accommodations made for children's food allergies.
NA permitted.

3.1 Schedule appropriate for children.

3.2 Well-balanced meals/snacks. *

3.3 Sanitary conditions usually maintained. *

3.4 Nonpunitive atmosphere during meals/snacks.

3.5 Allergies posted and food/beverage substitutions made. *
NA permitted.

3.6 Children with disabilities included at table with peers.
NA permitted.

5.1 Most staff sit with children during meals and group snacks. *

5.2 Pleasant social atmosphere.

5.3 Children are encouraged to eat independently (Ex. child-sized *eating* utensils provided; special spoon or cup for child with disabilities).

5.4 Dietary restrictions of families followed.
NA permitted.

7.1 Children help during meals/snacks (Ex. set table, serve themselves, clear table, wipe up spills).

7.2 Child-sized *serving* utensils used by children to make self-help easier (Ex. children use small pitcher, sturdy serving bowls and spoons).

7.3 Meals and snacks are times for conversation (Ex. staff encourage children to talk about events of day and talk about things children are interested in; children talk with one another).

(See Notes for Clarification and Question on next page)

1.2, 3.2. The intent of this indicator is to determine whether the correct components of a meal or snack are being served to the children. No analysis of the nutritional value of foods served is necessary. Use the USDA Meal Guidelines—ages 1–12, in *All About the ECERS-R*, p. 91, to determine whether the components are present. Personal dietary preferences of the assessor (e.g., preference for whole grain vs. white breads or fresh vs. canned vegetables) are not to be used in determining the quality of the foods served. As long as the required nutritionally adequate meals and snacks are served, within the acceptable timeframe (e.g., program less than or equal to 4 hours=1 meal or snack required; 4–6 hours=1 meal; 6–12 hours=2 meals and 1 snack or 2 snacks and 1 meal; more than 12 hours=2 snacks and 2 meals), credit can be given for 3.2. An occasional instance of not meeting the guidelines—for example, cupcakes for a birthday party instead of the scheduled snack—should not affect the rating. Any supplementary foods served in addition to the required meals/snacks do not have to meet the required components. Check menu for the week in addition to observing food served. If no menu is available, ask the teacher to describe meals/snacks served for the past week.

1.3. In the case where snack time is flexible and children come and go throughout a period of time, the same sanitary conditions are required (i.e., table sanitized between children using same places, children's hands washed). If children finger feed themselves during meals or hands become messy, then children should have hands washed after eating also.

3.3. If sanitary conditions are usually maintained and if handwashing and other sanitary procedures are clearly a part of the program, credit can be given for 3.3 even if there is an occasional lapse in practice.

3.5. A food/beverage substitution made in case of allergies or family dietary restrictions must meet the primary meal/snack nutrient contribution of the food/beverage it replaces. For example, in the case of milk, the substitute beverage needs to be equal in calcium and protein. Therefore, water, juice, or calcium-enriched juice is not a milk substitute since it does not replace the protein, but a vegetarian milk, such as soy milk, is. To get additional information in order to decide whether substitutes can be credited, ask staff, "How are substitutes made for foods/beverages children cannot eat?"

5.1. "Most" requires that it is *more likely* for staff to be sitting with the children during meals and group snacks than not. Although staff may need to leave the table to assist with the meal, most of the time should be spent sitting with the children. It is not required that each table have a staff member. Some staff may help with serving, while others sit with children.

Question

1.5, 3.5, 5.4. What do you do if children have food allergies or families have dietary restrictions?

Inadequate		Minimal		Good		Excellent
1	2	3	4	5	6	7

11. Nap/rest*

1.1 Nap/rest schedule is inappropriate for most of the children. *

1.2 Nap/rest provisions unsanitary (Ex. crowded area, dirty sheets, different children use same bedding).

1.3 Little supervision provided, or supervision is harsh.

3.1 Nap/rest is scheduled appropriately for most of the children (Ex. most children sleep).

3.2 Sanitary provisions for nap/rest (Ex. area not crowded, clean bedding). *

3.3 Sufficient supervision provided in the room throughout nap/rest. *

3.4 Calm, nonpunitive supervision.

5.1 Children helped to relax (Ex. cuddly toy, soft music, back rubbed).

5.2 Space is conducive to resting (Ex. dim light, quiet, cots placed for privacy).

5.3 All cots or mats are at least 3 feet apart or separated by a solid barrier.

7.1 Nap/rest schedule is flexible to meet individual needs (Ex. tired child given place to rest during play time).

7.2 Provisions made for early risers and non-nappers (Ex. early risers permitted to read books or play quietly; separate space and activities used for non-nappers). *

(See Notes for Clarification and Questions on next page)

Item 11. Score NA on this item for programs of 4 hours or less that do not provide a nap or rest. For longer programs, nap/rest should be based on the age and individual needs of the children.

1.1. "Inappropriate" schedule means that nap/rest is either too late or too early (e.g., children are tired long before naptime or are not ready to sleep), or children are left napping or required to be on their cots too long (more than 2½ hours), which might interfere with family bedtime routines.

3.2. "Not crowded" means the cots/mats are at least 18 inches apart, unless separated by a solid barrier. Children's bedding must be stored separately, so that personal items are not touching one another, mats/cots must be covered with material that makes them easy to wash and sanitize.

3.3. "Sufficient supervision" means enough staff are present to protect children's safety in case of emergency and handle children who wake up or need help. At least one alert staff member is always in the room.

7.2. Credit can be given when children can be happily occupied by reading a book or playing quietly while on their cots.

Questions

Could you describe how nap or rest is handled?

3.3. How is supervision handled at this time?

3.4, 7.2. What do you do if children are tired before naptime, have trouble settling down, or wake up early?

5.3. How far apart are cots or mats placed?

Inadequate		Minimal		Good		Excellent
1	2	3	4	5	6	7

12. Toileting/diapering

1.1 Sanitary conditions of area are not maintained (Ex. toilet/sinks dirty; diapering table/potty chairs not sanitized after each use, toilets rarely flushed). *

1.2 Lack of basic provisions interferes with care of children (Ex. no toilet paper or soap; same towel used by many children; no running water in area). *

1.3 Handwashing often neglected by staff or children after toileting/diapering. *

1.4 Inadequate or unpleasant supervision of children. *

3.1 Sanitary conditions are maintained. *

3.2 Basic provisions made for care of children.

3.3 Staff and children wash hands most of the time after toileting. *

3.4 Toileting schedule meets individual needs of children.

3.5 Adequate supervision for age and abilities of children. *

5.1 Sanitary conditions easy to maintain (Ex. no potty chairs used, warm running water near diapering table and toilets; easy to clean surfaces). *

5.2 Provisions convenient and accessible for children in group (Ex. steps near sink or toilet if needed; handrail for child with physical disability; toileting area adjacent to room).

5.3 Pleasant staff-child interaction.

7.1 Child-sized toilets and low sinks provided. *

7.2 Self-help skills promoted as children are ready.

(See Notes for Clarification on next page)

*Notes for Clarification

1.1, 3.1. If the same sink is used by either children or adults for both diapering/ toileting and food-related routines (including toothbrushing) or for other purposes (to wash toys/other classroom equipment; after wiping nose), it must be sanitized by spraying sink and faucets with a bleach solution after diapering/toileting use. As an exception to this rule, in order to avoid requiring children to wash hands in quick succession between toileting and being fed, the following applies: if children use toilet, wash hands and then immediately sit down for meal/snack, contamination of children's hands at toileting sink must be minimized by having children/adults turn off faucet with paper towel. Score 1.1 "No" if no major problems are observed, or only two or three minor problems. (For additional information on sanitation including proper diaper changing procedures, see *All About the ECERS-R*, pp. 111–114.)

1.2. In case special procedures are required such as diapering for an older child or catheterization, they must be handled in a sanitary manner that preserves the child's dignity.

1.3, 3.3. Assume that the handwashing seen during the observation is typical of what happens throughout the day. Base your ratings for 1.3 and 3.3 on what you see. Adults' hands must be washed even if gloves are used.

1.4. "Inadequate" supervision means that staff do not monitor to protect the safety of the children or to ensure that sanitary procedures (e.g., handwashing) are carried out.

3.1. Score "Yes" when no major problem is observed or only one minor problem is observed.

3.3. A score of "Yes" requires that 75% of children's hands are washed and 75% of adults hands are washed.

3.5. "Adequate" supervision means that teachers check to be sure that sanitary toilet conditions are maintained (e.g., toilets flushed, toilet paper/towels and soap provided) and ensure that children complete toileting procedures properly (e.g., wipe properly, wash hands, avoid inappropriate behaviors).

5.1. Since potty chairs are a health hazard, they should be avoided for general use. In the rare case when special need requires the use of a potty, credit toward a score of 5 may be given if the potty is used only for the child with a special need and is washed and disinfected after each use.

7.1. Child-sized sinks and toilets are fixtures that are considerably smaller or lower than regular-sized fixtures, and can be used comfortably by children without modifications such as toilet seats and steps. To give credit for 7.1, toilets and sinks must be usable with no adaptations (e.g., steps), by at least 75% of children in group.

Inadequate		Minimal		Good		Excellent
1	2	3	4	5	6	7

13. Health practices*

1.1 Staff usually do not act to cut down on the spread of germs (Ex. signs of animal contamination in outdoor or indoor play areas; noses not wiped; tissues not disposed of properly). *

1.2 Smoking is allowed in child care areas, either indoors or outdoors.

3.1 Adequate handwashing by staff and children takes place after wiping noses, after handling animals, or when otherwise soiled. *

3.2 Staff usually take action to cut down on the spread of germs. *

3.3 Smoking does not take place in child care areas.

3.4 Procedures used to minimize spread of contagious disease (Ex. ensuring children have immunizations; exclusion of children with contagious illness; TB tests for staff at least every 2 years). *

5.1 Children are dressed properly for conditions both indoors and outdoors (Ex. wet clothes changed on chilly day; warm clothes in cold weather).

5.2 Staff are good models of health practices (Ex. eat only healthful foods in front of children; check and flush toilets in children's bathroom).

5.3 Care given to children's appearance (Ex. faces washed, soiled clothes changed, aprons used for messy play).

7.1 Children taught to manage health practices independently (Ex. taught proper hand-washing techniques, to put on own coat or apron; reminded to flush toilet; health-related books, pictures, and games used).

7.2 Individual toothbrushes properly labeled and stored; used at least once during the day in full-day programs (Ex. toothbrushes are stored so they do not touch and brushes can be air dried). *
NA permitted.

(See Notes for Clarification and Questions on next page)

*Notes for Clarification

Item 13. This item excludes the sanitation procedures rated in Item 10. Meals/snacks, Item 11. Nap/rest, and Item 12. Toileting/diapering.

1.1. Areas where blood and other bodily fluid spills have occurred must be cleaned and disinfected. Gloves should be worn when handling blood.

3.1. "Adequate handwashing" means that hands are washed thoroughly with soap and running water, and dried with a towel that is not shared, or hands are air dried with a blower. Since handwashing at mealtimes and after toileting is rated in other items, rate here based on *all other* handwashing required. Give credit for 3.1 only if you observe that hands are washed 75% of times when needed. Wipes may be used when necessary, such as after wiping noses on the playground, but this is not counted as handwashing.

There are four categories of handwashing that must be tracked to score this indicator: (1) Upon arrival into classroom, and re-entering classroom after being outside, (2) Before and after water play or after messy play, (3) After dealing with bodily fluids, and (4) After touching contaminated objects and surfaces, such as trash can lids and pets. To score, observers should be aware of times that handwashing is carried out when needed. This means that the observer should watch (and listen). For example, observers should listen for coughing or sneezing by the children and staff, or watch for noses that need wiping to see that proper handwashing is carried out. Counts should be kept on the Score Sheet to indicate when handwashing has been carried out properly as needed, and when it has been ignored. (For sample handwashing tracking system see *All About the ECERS-R*, p. 125.)

3.1. (cont.) The 75% of required handwashing must be calculated separately for staff and children, but the percentage should be based on the total handwashing in all categories. If either group washes hands less than 75% of the time when needed, score 3.1 "No."

3.2. Examples for this indicator include: tissues available and used when necessary; same washcloth/towel not used for more than one child; soap available and used; toothbrushes stored to avoid contamination. "Usually take action" means 75% of the time. However, if there are any major problems, such as bodily fluid spills not cleaned up promptly or signs of animal contamination in children's play spaces, score 3.2 "No."

3.4. If a substantial number of these procedures are used to minimize spread of contagious diseases, give credit for this indicator. Not all examples in the indicator are required to score "Yes."

7.2. Score NA for programs open 6 hours or less per day. If the "same sink" is used for both tooth brushing and toileting, without sanitizing, consider this under Item 12. Toileting/diapering.

Questions

3.4. A general question such as "Do you have any health requirements for children and staff?" usually elicits the information needed to score. If not, add specific questions such as: How do you ensure that children have the necessary immunizations? Do you have rules for excluding children with contagious illnesses? Please describe. Are staff required to have TB tests? How often?

7.2. Do children brush their teeth? How is this handled? (Ask to see toothbrushes.)

Inadequate		Minimal		Good		Excellent
1	2	3	4	5	6	7

14. Safety practices

1.1 Several hazards that could result in serious injury indoors. *

1.2 Several hazards that could result in serious injury outdoors. *

1.3 Inadequate supervision to protect children's safety indoors and outdoors (Ex. too few staff; staff occupied with other tasks; no supervision near areas of potential danger; no check-in or check-out procedures). *

3.1 No major safety hazards indoors or outdoors. *

3.2 Adequate supervision to protect children's safety indoors and outdoors.

3.3 Essentials needed to handle emergencies available (Ex. telephone, emergency numbers, substitute for staff, first aid kit, transportation, written emergency procedures).

5.1 Staff anticipate and take action to prevent safety problems (Ex. remove toys under climbing equipment; lock dangerous areas to keep children out; wipe up spills to prevent falls).

5.2 Staff explain reasons for safety rules to children. *

7.1 Play areas are arranged to avoid safety problems (Ex. younger children play in separate playground or at a separate time; outdoor play equipment proper size and level of challenge).

7.2 Children generally follow safety rules (Ex. no crowding on slides, no climbing on bookcases).

(See Notes for Clarification and Question on next page)

1.1, 1.2, 3.1. The following list of major hazards is not meant to be complete. Be sure to note all safety problems on score sheet.

Some indoor safety problems:
- No safety caps on electrical sockets
- Loose electrical cords
- Heavy objects or furniture child can pull down
- Medicines, cleaning materials, and other substances labeled "keep out of reach of children" not locked away
- Pot handles on stove accessible
- Stove controls accessible
- Water temperature too hot
- Mats or rugs that slide
- Unprotected hot stove or fireplace in use
- Open stairwells accessible
- Play areas in front of doors

Some outdoor safety problems:
- Tools not meant for children's use are accessible
- Any substance labeled "keep out of reach of children" not locked away
- Sharp or dangerous objects present
- Unsafe walkways or stairs
- Easy access to road
- Hazardous trash accessible
- Play equipment too high, not well maintained, unanchored
- Play equipment poses threat of entrapment, injury from pinchpoints or projections

1.1. Score "Yes" when the observer can list two or more *very serious* hazards in indoor spaces used by the children or more than five minor hazards (such as loose carpet edge, splinters on a shelf, or bleach-water solution stored within children's reach). Bleach and water solution, used to sanitize surfaces, does not have to be locked away, but must be stored out of reach of young children. It should not be sprayed where it can be breathed in by children, for example, while children are seated around the table. Any electrical outlets or wires present where children are allowed to play must be safe (e.g., outlets covered, cords secure). When special safety outlets are used in a program, ask the teacher or director how they are operated to ensure child safety, and check to be sure operation rules are followed correctly. Flip covers on outdoor outlets are acceptable as safety caps as long as they are kept closed when not in use.

1.2. Score "Yes" when the observer can list two or more *very serious* hazards seen in the outdoor spaces used by children or six or more minor hazards (such as tree roots that are unlikely to cause tripping, shallow puddles, or sand on a sidewalk).

1.3. If this indicator is scored "Yes," then it is likely that Items 29 and 30 (supervision items) may also receive scores of 1. Note that to score this indicator "Yes," supervision must be inadequate both indoors *and* outdoors.

3.1. To give credit, there must be no more than five minor hazards observed.

5.2. To give credit, staff must be observed discussing or explaining safety rules.

Question

5.2. Do you talk about safety with children? What kinds of things do you discuss?

Inadequate		Minimal		Good		Excellent
1	2	3	4	5	6	7

LANGUAGE-REASONING

15. Books and pictures

1.1 Very few books accessible. *

1.2 Staff rarely read books to children (Ex. no daily story time, little individual reading to children). *

3.1 Some books accessible for children (Ex. during free play children have enough books to avoid conflict). *

3.2 At least one staff-initiated receptive language activity time daily (Ex. reading books to children, storytelling, using flannel board stories). *

5.1 A wide selection of books are accessible for a substantial portion of the day. *

5.2 Some additional language materials used daily. *

5.3 Books organized in a reading center.

5.4 Books, language materials, and activities are appropriate for children in group. *

5.5 Staff read books to children informally (Ex. during free play, at naptime, as an extension of an activity). *

7.1 Books and language materials are rotated to maintain interest.

7.2 Some books relate to current classroom activities or themes (Ex. books borrowed from library on seasonal theme). *

(See Notes for Clarification and Questions on next page)

*Notes for Clarification

1.1. Score "Yes" if fewer than five intact books are accessible to the children or if the accessible books can be used for less than 1 hour in a full-day program of 8 hours or more, appropriately prorated for shorter programs (see the chart in the "Explanation of Terms Used Throughout the Scale" on p. 7).

1.2. Score "Yes" if children are not read to at least once a day, except under unusual circumstances.

3.1. "Some books accessible" means that at least one book for half of the children allowed to attend at any time (e.g., 10 books for a group of 20). To give credit, books must be accessible for at least 1 hour per day in a program of 8 hours or more, appropriately prorated for shorter programs (see chart in "Explanation of Terms Used Throughout the Scale" on p. 7).

3.2. Reading may be done in small groups or in larger groups depending on the ability of the children to attend to the story.

5.1. All accessible books do not have to be found in the book area. Be sure to look for them in other areas of the room. A "wide selection of books" includes a variety of topics: *fantasy; factual information; stories about people, animals, and nature/science; books that reflect different cultures and abilities.* In order to be given credit for a wide selection there must be at least 20 books for a group of up to 15 children, and at least one extra book for each additional child over that number permitted to attend. *Approximately* 3–4 examples of each topic are required, but this rule is flexible, and there might be more or less of any topic. However, each topic must be represented. (See *All About the ECERS-R*, pp. 149–152, for further information.)

5.2. Examples of additional language materials are posters and pictures, flannel board stories, picture card games, and recorded stories and songs. To give credit, the materials must be accessible at least 1 hour daily in a full-day program of 8 hours or more, appropriately prorated for shorter programs (see chart in "Explanation of Terms Used Throughout the Scale" on p. 7).

5.4. Examples of "appropriate" materials and activities include simpler books read with younger children; large print materials for child with visual impairment; books in children's primary language(s); rhyming games for older children. If there are any books accessible to children that show violence in a graphic or frightening way, or that glorify violence, then credit cannot be given for this indicator. Check only books and pictures that are accessible to the children. It is not necessary to check materials that are not obviously meant as books/pictures for children such as stacks of magazines for use in art or materials not meant for use with children that are stored in a teacher's space.

5.5. Informal reading must be observed at least once to give credit for this indicator. (For examples of informal reading see *All About the ECERS-R*, pp. 154–155.)

7.2. Score "Yes" if three or more books relate to a theme studied during the past month. If themes are never changed, credit cannot be given.

Questions

7.1. Are there any other books used with the children? How is this handled?

7.2. How do you choose books?

16. Encouraging children to communicate*

1.1 No activities used by staff with children to encourage them to communicate (Ex. no talking about drawings, dictating stories, sharing ideas at circle time, finger plays, singing songs).

1.2 Very few materials accessible that encourage children to communicate. *

3.1 Some activities used by staff with children to encourage them to communicate. *

3.2 Some materials accessible to encourage children to communicate. *

3.3 Communication activities are generally appropriate for the children in the group. *

5.1 Communication activities take place during both free play and group times (Ex. child dictates story about painting; small group discusses trip to store).

5.2 Materials that encourage children to communicate are accessible in a variety of interest centers (Ex. small figures and animals in block area; puppets and flannel board pieces in book area; toys for dramatic play outdoors or indoors).

7.1 Staff balance listening and talking appropriately for age and abilities of children during communication activities (Ex. leave time for children to respond; verbalize for child with limited communication skills).

7.2 Staff link children's spoken communication with written language (Ex. write down what children dictate and read it back to them; help them write note to parents). *

---

*Notes for Clarification

Item 16. Children of different ages and abilities or those speaking a primary language different from the primary language of the classroom require different methods to encourage communication. Suitable activities must be included for children speaking a different primary language or those requiring alternative communication methods, such as signing or the use of augmentative communication devices.

1.2. Materials to encourage expressive language include play telephones, puppets, flannel board stories, dolls and dramatic play props, small figures and animals; communication boards and other assistive devices for children with disabilities. Score "Yes" if almost no materials are accessible for children to use, or accessibility of the materials is limited to a very short time period of the day, so that children rarely have a chance to use materials.

3.1. Activities used by staff to encourage children to communicate require that staff take action to draw communication from a child. During free play, for example, the teacher might ask the child to talk about what he or she is doing or making. During circle time, finger plays, songs, reciting nursery rhymes, or helping to tell a story would count toward meeting this indicator.

3.2. To give credit, the materials must be accessible for at least 1 hour per day in a program of 8 hours or more. For programs operating less than 8 hours, see chart in "Explanation of Terms Used Throughout the Scale" on p. 7 to determine the required amount of time.

3.3. Songs, poems, and/or chants, with violent, sexually explicit, or culturally biased content are considered inappropriate. Score this indicator, "No" if such material is observed in use.

7.2. Do *not* give credit for picture word labels on shelves or labels posted on other objects in the room. Also, if staff only write children's names on their work, no credit is given for this indicator, even if staff read names back to the children. (For examples of linking speaking to print, see *All About the ECERS-R*, pp. 165–167.)

Question

7.2. Do you do anything to help children see that what they say can be written down and read by others? Please give some examples.

Inadequate		Minimal		Good		Excellent
1	2	3	4	5	6	7

17. Using language to develop reasoning skills

1.1 Staff do not talk with children about logical relationships (Ex. ignore children's questions and curiosity about why things happen, do not call attention to sequence of daily events, differences and similarity in number, size, shape; cause and effect).

1.2 Concepts are introduced inappropriately (Ex. concepts too difficult for age and abilities of children; inappropriate teaching methods used such as worksheets without any concrete experiences; teacher gives answers without helping children to figure things out). *

3.1 Staff sometimes talk about logical relationships or concepts (Ex. explain that outside time comes after snacks, point out differences in sizes of blocks child used). *

3.2 Some concepts are introduced appropriately for ages and abilities of children in group, using words and concrete experiences (Ex. guide children with questions and words to sort big and little blocks or to figure out the cause for ice melting). *

5.1 Staff talk about logical relationships while children play with materials that stimulate reasoning (Ex. sequence cards, same/different games, size and shape toys, sorting games, number and math games). *

5.2 Children encouraged to talk through or explain their reasoning when solving problems (Ex. why they sorted objects into different groups; in what way are two pictures the same or different). *

7.1 Staff encourage children to reason throughout the day, using actual events and experiences as a basis for concept development (Ex. children learn sequence by talking about their experiences in the daily routine or recalling the sequence of a cooking project). *

7.2 Concepts are introduced in response to children's interests or needs to solve problems (Ex. talk children through balancing a tall block building; help children figure out how many spoons are needed to set table). *

*Notes for Clarification

1.2. Concepts include same/different, matching, classifying, sequencing, one-to-one correspondence, spatial relationships, cause and effect.

3.1. "Staff sometimes talk about logical relationships" means that during the observation staff are observed making comments that relate to logical concepts at least *twice*.

3.2. If at least two instances are observed during the observation, score "Yes".

5.1. At least one instance must be observed.

5.2. At least two instances must be observed.

7.1. To give credit, at least two examples must be observed that are not related to children's use of play materials that encourage reasoning.

7.2. At least two instances must be observed.

Inadequate		Minimal		Good		Excellent
1	2	3	4	5	6	7

18. Informal use of language*

1.1 Staff talk to children only to control their behavior and manage routines.

1.2 Staff rarely respond to children's talk.

1.3 Children's talk is discouraged much of the day.

3.1 Some staff-child conversation (Ex. ask "yes/no" or short answer questions; give short answers to children's questions). *

3.2 Children allowed to talk much of the day.

5.1 Many staff-child conversations during free play and routines.

5.2 Language is primarily used by staff to exchange information with children and for social interaction. *

5.3 Staff add information to expand on ideas presented by children. *

5.4 Staff encourage communication among children, including those with disabilities (Ex. remind children to listen to one another; teach all children to sign if classmate uses sign language).

7.1 Staff have individual conversations with most of the children. *

7.2 Children are asked questions to encourage them to give longer and more complex answers. (Ex. young child is asked "what" or "where" questions; older child is asked "why" or "how" questions). *

---

*Notes for Clarification

Item 18. When multiple staff are working with the children, base the score for this item on the overall impact of the staff's communication with the children. The intent of this item is that children's need for language stimulation is met.

3.1. In order to be given credit for "conversation," there should be some mutual listening and talking/responding from both the staff and child. This is different from one-way communication such as giving directions or commands. For children with less verbal ability, the response may not be in words but may involve gestures, sign language, or communication devices.

5.2. In order to decide on a score for this indicator, consider the amount of language staff use to manage routines and control behavior in relationship to the amount of language used to exchange information and interact socially. If a far greater amount is used for information exchange and social discussion (about 75%) than for control and management, score "Yes."

5.3. "Expand" means staff respond verbally to add more information to what a child says. For example, a child says, "Look at this truck," and the teacher responds, "It's a red dump truck. See, it has a place to carry things." Observe to see if staff use many words in response to children's interests. When a child with restricted verbal ability points to something, if staff only name the object, do not give credit. Give credit, if in addition to the name, staff add more information, (e.g., color and other properties of object, use, etc.). Credit can be given if the staff initiates the topic and then adds to what the child says in response to the question. At least two instances of expansion must be observed during the observation.

7.1, 7.2. To give credit for these indicators, several instances must be observed.

Inadequate		Minimal		Good		Excellent
1	2	3	4	5	6	7

ACTIVITIES

19. Fine motor

1.1 Very few developmentally appropriate fine motor materials accessible for daily use.

1.2 Fine motor materials generally in poor repair or incomplete (Ex. puzzles have missing pieces, few pegs for pegboard). *

3.1 Some developmentally appropriate fine motor materials of each type accessible. *

3.2 Most of the materials are in good repair and complete. *

5.1 Many developmentally appropriate fine motor materials of each type accessible for a substantial portion of the day. *

5.2 Materials are well organized (Ex. pegs and pegboards stored together, building toy sets stored separately).

5.3 Materials on different levels of difficulty accessible (Ex. both regular and knobbed puzzles for children with varying fine motor skills).

7.1 Materials rotated to maintain interest (Ex. materials that are no longer of interest put away, different materials brought out).

7.2 Containers and accessible storage shelves have labels to encourage self-help (Ex. pictures or shapes used as labels on containers and shelves; word labels added for older children). *

---

*Notes for Clarification

1.2. "Generally in poor repair or incomplete" means 80% of materials cannot be used properly because pieces are missing, parts are broken, or there are other problems.

3.1. There are several different types of fine motor materials, including *small building toys* such as interlocking blocks and Lincoln logs; *art materials* such as crayons and scissors; *manipulatives* such as beads of different sizes for stringing, pegs and pegboards, sewing cards; and *puzzles*. "Some" of each type means more than one example of each of the four types is accessible for 1 hour in an 8-hour program, prorated appropriately in shorter programs (see "Explanation of Terms Used Throughout the Scale" on p. 7 for amount of time required). In order to be given credit for one example of a type, the material must be complete and in good enough condition to permit the activity for which it was designed. Therefore, crayons and paper to draw on is one example of an art material, a puzzle with all its pieces is one example of puzzles, a set of beads with strings is one example of manipulatives. (For further details about the four types of fine motor materials see *All About the ECERS-R,* pp. 189, 190.)

3.2. "Most" means 80% of fine motor materials.

5.1. "Many" requires at least three examples of each type to be accessible for a substantial portion of the day. Many items representing each type do not all have to be accessible at the same time, however a combination of these materials needs to be accessible for a substantial portion of the day to assure that children have a wide choice.

7.2. To give credit, almost all shelves and/or containers must have labels that are meaningful to the children.

Questions

5.1. When are the manipulatives and other fine motor materials accessible for children to use?

7.1. Do you use any other fine motor materials with children? How is this handled?

39

Inadequate		Minimal		Good		Excellent
1	2	3	4	5	6	7

20. Art*

1.1 Art activities are rarely available to the children. *

1.2 No individual expression in art activities (Ex. coloring work sheets; teacher-directed projects where children are asked to copy an example). *

3.1 Some art materials accessible for at least 1 hour a day. *

3.2 Some individual expression permitted with art materials (Ex. children allowed to decorate pre-cut shapes in their own way; in addition to teacher-directed projects, some individualized work is permitted). *

5.1 Many and varied art materials accessible a substantial portion of the day. *

5.2 Much individual expression in use of art materials (Ex. projects that follow an example are rarely used; children's work is varied and individual). *

7.1 Three-dimensional art materials included at least monthly (Ex. clay, play dough, wood gluing, carpentry).

7.2 Some art activities are related to other classroom experiences (Ex. paints in fall colors when learning about seasons; children invited to do picture following field trip).

7.3 Provisions made for children four and older to extend art activity over several days (Ex. project stored so work can continue; work on multi-step projects encouraged).
NA permitted.

(See Notes for Clarification and Questions on next page)

Item 20. Categories of art materials: *drawing materials* such as paper, crayons, nontoxic felt pens, thick pencils; *paints; three-dimensional materials* such as play dough, clay, wood gluing, or carpentry; *collage materials; tools* such as safe scissors, staplers, hole punches, tape dispensers.

1.1. "Rarely available" means activities with art materials are offered less than once a day, or if offered daily, all children do not have the opportunity to participate if they wish, or the time offered is too short to be satisfying to the children.

1.2, 3.2. "Individual expression" means that each child may select the subject matter and/or art medium, and carry out the work in his or her own way. A number of paintings, each of which is different because the children have not been asked to imitate a model or assigned a subject to paint, is considered "individual expression."

3.1. In groups with children under 3 years of age or with certain developmental delays, staff may bring out materials to make them accessible daily with close supervision for as long as there is interest. Adaptations may be needed to make art materials accessible and usable for children with disabilities. "Some" means at least one usable art material that will allow children to complete artwork (e.g., crayons with paper). To give credit, the materials must be accessible daily for at least 1 hour in an 8 hour program, prorated appropriately for shorter programs (see chart in "Explanation of Terms Used Throughout the Scale" on p. 7).

5.1. "Many and varied" requires that 3-5 different art materials be accessible from at least four of the categories for a substantial portion of the day, and drawing materials is required as one of the four. All categories need not be accessible at the same time, as long as each is included for some time during the substantial portion of the day. (For more information about the categories, see *All About the ECERS-R*, p. 200.) Food cannot be counted as an art material.

5.2. "Much individual expression" means that 85% of the time when art materials are used, children can do "free art" and are not required to follow an example. Observe to see whether children have access to the art materials and if they actually use them in their own creative way. You may also look at the artwork displayed in the room. If you see many teacher-directed projects displayed, and little individual work being done by the children during the observation, do not give credit for this indicator. If you are not sure, ask the teacher how often projects like those in the display are done. If projects that meet the requirements of 3.2 are used no more than once or twice a week, and you observe many instances of children using art materials in their own, creative way, you may give credit for 5.2, even if much of the work displayed is of the "project" variety. (For further discussion of individual expression requirements at the 3 and 5 levels, see *All About the ECERS-R*, pp. 201–204.)

Questions

5.2. How do you choose what to put on the bulletin board?

7.1. Are three-dimensional art materials such as clay or wood for gluing, ever used? If so, how often?

7.2. How do you choose what art activities to offer the children?

7.3. Do you offer art activities that children can work on over several days? Please describe some examples.

Inadequate		Minimal		Good		Excellent
1	2	3	4	5	6	7

21. Music/movement

1.1 No music/movement experiences for children.

1.2 Loud background music is on much of the day and interferes with ongoing activities (Ex. constant background music makes conversation in normal tones difficult; music raises noise level).

3.1 Some music materials accessible for children's use (Ex. simple instruments; music toys; tape player with tapes). *

3.2 Staff initiate at least one music activity daily (Ex. sing songs with children; soft music put on at naptime, play music for dancing).

3.3 Some movement/dance activity done at least weekly (Ex. marching or moving to music; acting out movements to songs or rhymes; children given scarves and encouraged to dance to music).

5.1 Many music materials accessible for children's use (Ex. music center with instruments, tape player, dance props; adaptations made for children with disabilities). *

5.2 Various types of music are used with the children (Ex. classical and popular music; music characteristic of different cultures; some songs sung in different languages). *

7.1 Music available as both a free choice and group activity daily.

7.2 Music activities that extend children's understanding of music are offered occasionally (Ex. guest invited to play instrument; children make musical instruments; staff set up activity to help children hear different tones). *

7.3 Creativity is encouraged with music activities (Ex. children asked to make up new words to songs; individual dance encouraged).

(See Notes for Clarification and Questions on next page)

3.1. "Some" means more than one example of music materials are accessible for at least 1 hour per day in an 8-hour program, prorated appropriately for shorter programs (see "Explanation of Terms Used Throughout the Scale" on p. 7 for time required in shorter program). The materials need not be accessible at the same time.

5.1. To give credit for "many," there must be enough musical instruments for at least half of the children to use at once *plus* some music to listen to, such as a tape player with tapes or a computer program that has extensive musical content (e.g., complete songs, and/or passages of music). Do not give credit for very short musical sound patterns on the computer, as found in many computer games. Dance props must be accompanied by something that makes music such as recorded music, child-created music, or adult created music. For a tape player to be considered accessible in a group of older children (majority of children are 4 years and older), children should be able to use the tapes independently, but in younger groups help may be needed from the teacher.

5.1. (cont.) To give credit, the "many" music materials must be *accessible* for at least 1 hour daily in programs operating 8 hours or more a day. Less time is required for programs operating less than 8 hours a day, with the amount of time calculated proportionally, based on the ratio of 1 hour for programs of 8 hours or more (see "Explanation of Terms Used Throughout the Scale" on p. 7 for time required for shorter programs).

5.2. "Various types of music" means at least three different types. (See *All About the ECERS-R*, p. 216 for a list of types of music.)

7.2. For this indicator, "occasionally" means at least 3–4 times per year.

Questions

How do you handle music with the children?

3.2. How often do you do music activities with the children?

3.3. Do children ever do movement or dance activities? About how often is this done?

5.2. What kinds of music do you use with the children?

7.2. Do you ever do special music activities?

7.3. Are there any opportunities for children to do music activities in their own way?

Inadequate		Minimal		Good		Excellent
1	2	3	4	5	6	7

22. Blocks*

1.1 Few blocks are accessible for children's play. *

3.1 Enough blocks and accessories are accessible for at least two children to build independent structures at the same time. *

3.2 Some clear floor space used for block play.

3.3 Blocks and accessories accessible for daily use. *

5.1 Enough space, blocks, and accessories are accessible for three or more children to build at the same time. *

5.2 Blocks and accessories are organized according to type.

5.3 Special block area set aside out of traffic, with storage and suitable building surface (Ex. flat rug or other steady surface). *

5.4 Block area accessible for play for a substantial portion of the day. *

7.1 At least two types of blocks and a variety of accessories accessible daily (Ex. large and small; homemade and commercial).

7.2 Blocks and accessories are stored on open, labeled shelves (Ex. labeled with picture or outline of blocks). *

7.3 Some block play available outdoors.

(See Notes for Clarification and Questions on next page)

Item 22. Blocks are materials suitable for building sizable structures. Types of blocks are *unit blocks* (wooden or plastic, including shapes such as rectangles, squares, triangles, and cylinders); *large hollow blocks* (wooden, plastic, or cardboard); *homemade blocks* (materials such as food boxes and plastic containers). Note that interlocking blocks (whether large or small, indoors or outdoors) are not considered blocks for this item, but are given credit under Item 19. Fine motor. Usually the block area will be found in the classroom being observed. However, in a center where there is a block area that is outside the observed classroom (such as in a multi-purpose room or outdoors), that is accessible to the children on a regular basis, this should be considered when scoring this item.

1.1. "Few blocks" means there are no blocks for children to use or fewer blocks than are needed for two children to each build a sizable structure.

3.1. "Enough blocks" means there are sufficient blocks of a specific type that can be used together to make a sizable structure. Random collections of blocks with fewer than 10–20 of each type cannot be given credit because they are difficult to build with. To give credit, block "accessories" need to be within or near the block area so that it is obvious to the children that those materials are to be used with the blocks. Accessories enrich block play. Examples are toy people, animals, vehicles, and road signs. If accessories are not stored near or with the blocks, it must be observed that children actually use the materials as block accessories. If not observed, then credit cannot be given.

3.3. To give credit, blocks and accessories must be accessible for one hour in programs of 8 hours or more, prorated for programs operating fewer hours (see "Explanation of Terms Used Throughout the Scale" p. 7).

5.1. This indicator requires enough blocks for three children to build sizable structures independently. Observe how space for block play is used. No specific square footage is required. If you don't observe children using this area, then imagine how it would be used based on the size of the block area and type of blocks. Also consider age and ability of children.

5.3. The block area may include other types of small and interlocking blocks considered under Item 19. Fine motor, in addition to blocks, and still be given credit for being a special block area. Usually, credit cannot be given if other materials, such as other fine motor toys, art, pretend play materials, or carpentry tools are included with the blocks and interfere with block play in any way. However, if there are a few hardhats or small toy houses/buildings in the block area that do not take up space, or interfere with block play, credit can be given.

5.4. All block areas considered in calculating accessibility for a substantial part of the day must meet requirements of 5.1–5.3. Additional block areas may be outdoors or in another indoor space.

7.2. When labeling block shelves, use of printed words only without the graphic representation of blocks is not given credit.

Questions

3.3. How often is block play available? About how long are the blocks available for play?

7.3. Do the children play with blocks outdoors?

Inadequate		Minimal		Good		Excellent
1	2	3	4	5	6	7

23. Sand/water*

1.1 No provision for sand *or* water play, outdoors *or* indoors. *

1.2 No toys to use for sand *or* water play.

3.1 Some provision for sand *or* water play accessible either outdoors *or* indoors. *

3.2 Some sand/water toys accessible.

5.1 Provision for sand *and* water play (either outdoors *or* indoors).

5.2 Variety of toys accessible for play (Ex. containers, spoons, funnels, scoops, shovels, pots and pans, molds, toy people, animals, and trucks). *

5.3 Sand *or* water play available to children for at least 1 hour daily. *

7.1 Provision for sand *and* water play, *both* indoors *and* outdoors (weather permitting). *

7.2 Different activities done with sand and water (Ex. bubbles added to water, material in sand table changed, i.e. rice substituted for sand).

(See Notes for Clarification and Questions on next page)

Item 23. Materials that can easily be poured, such as rice, lentils, birdseed, and cornmeal may be substituted for sand. Sand or sand substitute must be available in sufficient quantity so children can dig in it, fill containers, and pour. Woodchips can be considered a substitute for sand if the material can be used in the same way as sand—that is, easily poured or dug in—and if children would not get splinters when using the material. Health or safety issues related to use of sand, water, or sand substitutes should be considered in Items 13 and 14.

1.1. "Provision" for sand and water requires action on the part of staff to provide appropriate materials for such play. Allowing children to play in puddles or dig in the dirt on the playground does not meet the requirements of this item.

3.1. Each room does not have to have its own sand and water table, but must be able to use a sand and water table regularly if it is shared with another room. To give credit, access does not need to be provided on a daily basis, but should be a regular part of the program, for example, at least for ½ hour twice a week.

5.2. For "variety," consider the *differences among the toys* that children can use. Variety is represented in toy characteristics, such as use, size, transparency level, shape, color, and these types of properties should be considered, but *use* of the toys is of prime importance in making a scoring decision. If only duplicates of one toy are accessible (e.g., many spoons), then the requirements for variety are not met. Variety in toys does not have to be provided all at one time—variety can be provided through regular rotation of toys.

5.2. (cont.) If the teacher reports that toys are rotated, ask to see the other toys, and find out how often they are rotated. If both sand and water are accessible, variety in toys must be provided for both, but the same toys can be used to meet the requirement.

Number of toys accessible for play is also considered when determining "variety." For example, when fewer children use the toys at one time, fewer toys are required for variety, as long as the toys can be used for different purposes. When more children must share, more toys of different types are needed.

5.3. For programs of 4 hours or less, the requirement of 1 hour is changed to ½ hour.

7.1. Separate provisions for indoor use and outdoor use for sand and water play must be provided to give credit for this indicator. Giving credit cannot depend on a teacher's moving one provision (e.g., a sand/water table) from indoors to outdoors every day. Because of the inconvenience for the teacher and the difficulty of changing the material in the one container to allow for the provision of *both* sand and water, dual use of one piece of equipment is unlikely to occur often.

Questions

3.1. Do you use sand or water with the children? How is this handled? About how often? Where is this available?

3.2. Are there any toys for children to use with sand or water play? Please describe them.

7.2. Do you change the activities children do with sand and water?

Inadequate		Minimal		Good		Excellent
1	2	3	4	5	6	7

24. Dramatic play*

1.1 No materials or equipment accessible for dress up or dramatic play.

3.1 Some dramatic play materials and furniture accessible, so children can act out family roles themselves (Ex. dress-up clothes, housekeeping props, dolls).

3.2 Materials are accessible for at least 1 hour daily. *

3.3 Separate storage for dramatic play materials.

5.1 Many dramatic play materials accessible, including dress-up clothes. *

5.2 Materials accessible for a substantial portion of the day. *

5.3 Props for at least two different themes accessible daily (Ex. housekeeping and work). *

5.4 Dramatic play area clearly defined, with space to play and organized storage. *

7.1 Materials rotated for a variety of themes (Ex. prop boxes for work, fantasy, and leisure themes).

7.2 Props provided to represent diversity (Ex. props representing various cultures; equipment used by people with disabilities). *

7.3 Props provided for active dramatic play outdoors. *

7.4 Pictures, stories, and trips used to enrich dramatic play.

(See Notes for Clarification and Questions on next page)

Item 24. Dramatic play is pretending or making believe. This type of play occurs when children act out roles themselves and when they manipulate figures such as small toy people in a dollhouse. Thus, activities used to teach children to follow specific sequences to properly complete household chores, such as table washing or silver polishing activities, are not counted to meet the requirements of this item. Children must be free to use the materials in their own way, as part of their own make-believe play, to get credit for this item.

Dramatic play is enhanced by props that encourage a variety of themes including *housekeeping* (e.g., dolls, child-sized furniture, dress-up, kitchen utensils); *different kinds of work* (e.g., office, construction, farm, store, fire-fighting, transportation); *fantasy* (e.g., animals, dinosaurs, storybook characters); and *leisure* (e.g., camping, sports).

3.2. To give credit, the materials must be *accessible* for at least 1 hour daily in programs operating 8 hours or more. Less time is required for programs operating less than 8 hours a day, with the amount of time calculated proportionally (see "Explanation of Terms Used Throughout the Scale" on p. 7 for time required for shorter programs).

5.1. "Many" dramatic play materials means that three or more children can use the materials at one time, without undue competition, and the materials are plentiful enough to encourage more complex play. Dress-up clothes are required as part of the "many" materials, but many examples of dress-up clothes are not required. Hats, purses, and shoes count as dress-up clothes. However, since children are developing gender-role identity during the preschool years, they require concrete examples of dress-ups that are associated with being men or women. Thus, two or three gender-specific examples of dress-up items are required (such as ties, hard hats, or shoes to represent men's clothes; purses or flowery hats for women's). More generic clothing, such as sweatshirts or running shoes, can also be provided, but these do not count as gender-specific dress-ups.

5.2. Consider materials both indoors and outdoors when calculating accessibility for a substantial portion of the day. Dress-up clothes, required in 5.1, are not required for outdoor dramatic play because they might be dangerous. However, props outside must be complete enough to permit meaningful pretend play. For example, an outdoor house must have furniture and other props, doll strollers must have dolls, kitchen furniture must have things to use in a kitchen, child-sized riding cars should have a gas pump or things to transport, cars in the sandbox should have a toy garage or people.

5.3. Consider small toys that children can pretend with, both indoors and outdoors, when scoring this indicator (e.g., small dolls, trucks, animals). (For further discussion about dramatic play themes see *All About the ECERS-R*, pp. 239–241.)

5.4. Organized storage means that materials of the same type (e.g., dolls, dress-ups, cooking props, food props) are generally stored together (e.g., in containers or in furniture). Storage does not have to be perfectly neat.

7.2. Consider dolls of different races, cultures, ages, and abilities as props for this indicator, as well as dress-up clothes, play foods, and cooking utensils representing different cultures.

7.3. The intent of this indicator is that children are provided a large enough space so that their dramatic play can be very active and noisy without disrupting other activities. A large indoor space such as a gymnasium or multi-purpose room may be substituted for the outdoor space. Structures (such as small houses, cars, or boats) and props for camping, cooking, work, transportation, or dress-up clothes may be available to the children.

Questions

7.1. Are there any other dramatic play props children can use? Please describe them.

7.3. Are props for dramatic play ever used outside or in a larger indoor space?

7.4. Is there anything you do to extend children's dramatic play?

Inadequate		Minimal		Good		Excellent
1	2	3	4	5	6	7

25. Nature/science*

1.1 No games, materials, or activities for nature/science accessible.

3.1 Some developmentally appropriate games, materials, or activities from two nature/science categories accessible. *

3.2 Materials accessible daily. *

3.3 Children encouraged to bring in natural things to share with others or add to collections (Ex. bring fall leaves in from playground; bring in pet).

5.1 Many developmentally appropriate games, materials, and activities from three categories accessible. *

5.2 Materials are accessible for a substantial portion of the day. *

5.3 Nature/science materials are well organized and in good condition (Ex. collections stored in separate containers, animals' cages clean).

5.4 Everyday events used as a basis for learning about nature/science (Ex. talking about the weather, observing insects or birds, discussing the change of seasons, blowing bubbles or flying kites on a windy day, watching snow melt and freeze). *

7.1 Nature/science activities requiring more input from staff are offered at least once every 2 weeks (Ex. cooking, simple experiments like measuring rainfall, field trips).

7.2 Books, pictures, and/or audio/visual materials used to add information and extend children's hands-on experiences.

(See Notes for Clarification and Questions on next page)

*Notes for Clarification

Item 25. Nature/science materials include the following categories: ***collections of natural objects*** (e.g., rocks, insects, seed pods), ***living things*** to care for and observe (e.g., house plants, gardens, pets), ***nature/science books, games,*** or ***toys*** (e.g., nature matching cards, nature sequence cards), and ***nature/science activities*** such as cooking and simple experiments (e.g., with magnets, magnifying glasses, sink-and-float). The term *collections of natural objects* requires that there are groups of similar objects that can be classified together. For example, look for a collection of seashells, fall seeds, leaves, pinecones. Sufficient numbers of the objects in each collection must be present to allow children to explore similarities and/or differences. The collections must be of natural things; plastic collections (e.g., insects, zoo animals) are counted as science/nature toys. Collections must be accessible to the children if they are to count towards meeting indicator 5.2, requiring a substantial portion of the day.

3.1. Open-ended nature/science materials that children can explore in their own way are usually developmentally appropriate for a wide range of ages and abilities. Materials that require skills beyond the ability of individual children or that do not challenge children sufficiently are not developmentally appropriate. For example, having children fill in the height of the red line on a thermometer to tell hot from cold may be appropriate for kindergartners but not for 2-year-olds.

3.2. Materials must be accessible for at least 1 hour in a program of 8 hours or longer, prorated for shorter programs (see "Explanation of Terms Used Throughout the Scale" on p. 7).

5.1. "Many" means *approximately* 3–5 examples of three categories of nature/science materials. However, this can vary as long as three of the four categories are represented. In some cases you might give credit for more than 3–5 of one type and less than 3–5 of another. This will also depend on the ages and number of children in the group. (For a description of each of the four categories of nature/science materials, see *All About the ECERS-R*, pp. 253–256.)

5.2. Consider materials both indoors and outdoors when calculating accessibility for a substantial portion of the day. Requirements for 5.1 must be met in order to give credit for 5.2. If outdoor time is included in calculating substantial portion of the day, materials from at least two categories must be accessible during outdoor time.

5.4. Must observe one example or see clear evidence (e.g., photos, drawings). (For examples of everyday events see *All About the ECERS-R*, pp. 259–260.)

Questions

3.3. Do children bring in nature or science things to share? How do you handle this?

7.1. Can you give me some examples of nature/science activities you do with the children in addition to what I've seen? About how often are these activities done?

7.2. Do you use nature/science books or AV materials with the children? Please describe.

Inadequate		Minimal		Good		Excellent
1	2	3	4	5	6	7

26. Math/number*

1.1 No math/number materials accessible.

1.2 Math/number taught primarily through rote counting or worksheets. *

3.1 Some developmentally appropriate math/number materials accessible. *

3.2 Materials accessible daily. *

5.1 Many developmentally appropriate materials of various types accessible (Ex. materials for counting, measuring, learning shape and size). *

5.2 Materials are accessible for a substantial portion of the day.

5.3 Materials are well organized and in good condition (Ex. sorted by type, all pieces needed for games stored together). *

5.4 Daily activities used to promote math/number learning (Ex. setting table, counting while climbing steps, using timers to take turns). *

7.1 Math/number activities requiring more input from staff are offered at least every 2 weeks (Ex. making a chart to compare children's height, counting and recording number of birds at bird feeder). *

7.2 Materials are rotated to maintain interest (Ex. teddy bear counters replaced by dinosaur counters, different objects to weigh).

(See Notes for Clarification and Questions on next page)

Item 26. Different types of materials for math/number help children to experience *counting*, *measuring*, *comparing quantities*, *recognizing shapes*, and to become familiar with *written numbers*. Examples of math/number materials are: small objects to count, balance scales, rulers, number puzzles, magnetic numbers, number games such as dominoes or number lotto, and geometric shapes such as parquetry blocks.

1.2. "Taught primarily through rote counting or worksheets" means that such experiences make up the vast majority of children's math/number learning opportunities.

3.1. Developmentally appropriate math/number materials allow children to use concrete objects to experiment with quantity, size, and shape as they develop the concepts they need for the more abstract tasks required later in school, such as adding, subtracting, and completing paper and pencil math problems. Whether a material or activity is appropriate is based on the abilities and interests of the children. An occasional math worksheet offered to kindergartners who have many other concrete materials to manipulate may be developmentally appropriate for them, but not for 2- and 3-year-olds. Look around the room carefully to find math materials because they might not be organized into a center. "Some" means at least two different materials from at least three of the five types listed. (For a list of examples of the categories of math materials see *All About the ECERS-R*, pp. 267–269.)

3.2. To give credit, materials must be accessible for 1 hour in programs of 8 hours or more, prorated for programs operating fewer hours (see "Explanation of Terms Used Throughout the Scale," p. 7).

5.1. "Many" means *approximately* 3–5 of each type. However, this can vary, as long as all four types are represented. In some cases you might give credit for more than 3–5 of one type and less than 3–5 of another. This will also depend on the ages and number of children in the group. Credit should be given for materials obviously designed for math learning (e.g., puzzle with graduated sizes or different shapes, pegboard with number printed and holes to match, balance scale with things to weigh, nested cups that require size recognition). To give credit for more generic materials (blocks, beads for stringing, sets of bears with many pieces), it must be observed that the materials are used for math learning.

5.3. In order to give credit for "well organized and in good condition," about 75% of the materials that are accessible should meet this standard.

5.4. The intent of this indicator is for adults to link math and numbers to practical life events in the children's daily schedule. Therefore, look for use of numbers during meals or getting ready for meals (such as setting the table), transition times, using a timer to take turns, counting who is absent, etc. Do not give credit for play activities such as number games or computer games in determining the score for this indicator. "Number talk" or number experiences as part of practical life events should be observed *more than once* during the observation to give credit for this indicator. (For examples of number talk see *All About the ECERS-R*, pp. 272, 273.)

7.1. For a list of activities see *All About the ECERS-R*, pp. 273, 274.

Questions

7.1. Could you give me some examples of math activities you do with the children in addition to what I've seen?

7.2. Are there any other math materials used with the children? How is this handled?

Inadequate		Minimal		Good		Excellent
1	2	3	4	5	6	7

27. Use of TV, video, and/or computers*

1.1 Materials used are not developmentally appropriate (Ex. violent or sexually explicit content, frightening characters or stories, computer game too difficult). *

1.2 No alternative activity is allowed while TV/computer is being used (Ex. all children must watch video program at same time).

3.1 All materials used are nonviolent and culturally sensitive. *

3.2 Alternative activities accessible while TV/computer is being used.

3.3 Time children allowed to use TV/video or computer is limited (Ex. TV/videos limited to one hour daily in full-day program; computer turns limited to 20 minutes daily). *

5.1 Materials used are limited to those considered "good for children" (Ex. Sesame Street, educational video and computer games, but not most cartoons). *

5.2 Computer used as one of many free choice activities.
NA permitted.

5.3 Most of the materials encourage active involvement (Ex. children can dance, sing, or exercise to video; computer software encourages children to think and make decisions).

5.4 Staff are actively involved in use of TV, video, or computer (Ex. watch and discuss video with children; do activity suggested in educational TV program; help child learn to use computer program).

7.1 Some of the computer software encourages creativity (Ex. creative drawing or painting program, opportunities to solve problems in computer game).
NA permitted.

7.2 Materials used to support and extend classroom themes and activities (Ex. CD ROM or video on insects adds information on nature theme; video on farms prepares children for fieldtrip).

(See Notes for Clarification and Questions on next page)

Item 27. If neither TV, video, nor computer is used, score the item NA (Not Applicable). You must always ask about the use of TV and computers as they are often shared by several classrooms and may not be evident on the day of your visit. If TV/video are used very infrequently, less than once a month, and only for relatively short periods during which all children are interested, mark this item NA. However, even if TV is used infrequently, but for longer periods at a time, causing problems for the children, score the item as written.

1.1, 3.1. To judge whether materials are non-violent and culturally sensitive, consider the content of the materials. Unfortunately, many children's videos or TV programs contain violence and are therefore inappropriate even though they have been created for the children's market. This may include some natural wildlife productions and cartoons. The appropriateness of videos or games brought from children's homes also must be judged, if these materials are used with the group of children.

3.3. The intent of this indicator is to ensure that children participate in play in which they can actively be creative, imaginative, and have hands-on experiences with real materials rather than spending inordinate amounts of time watching TV or playing computer games. The amount of time given in the example is a general indication of a required time limitation and can vary. When deciding whether adequate limits are set on amount of time children can use the computer, consider not just how long each child's turn is, but also the number of turns each child is allowed to have, and if children spend time watching others at the computer. Computer time should be relatively short, compared to other activities.

5.1. Materials that are developed specifically to enhance children's learning and understanding are considered to be more educational and "good for children." (For examples see *All About the ECERS-R*, p. 282.)

Questions

Are TV, videos, or computers used with the children? How are they used?

1.1, 3.1, 5.1, 7.1. How do you choose the TV, video, or computer materials to use with the children? Are staff familiar with the content of materials before allowing use in the program? Are requirements for appropriateness considered before showing materials brought from home?

1.2, 3.2. Are other activities available to children while TV or videos are used?

3.3. How often are TV, video, or computers used with the children? For what length of time are these available?

5.3. Do any of the materials encourage active involvement by the children? Please give some examples.

7.2. Do you use TV, video, or the computer related to topics or themes in the classroom? Please explain.

Inadequate		Minimal		Good		Excellent
1	2	3	4	5	6	7

28. Promoting acceptance of diversity*

1.1 No racial or cultural diversity visible in materials (Ex. all toys and pictures are of one race, all print materials are about one culture, all print and audio materials are in one language where bilingualism is prevalent).

1.2 Materials present only stereotypes of races, cultures, ages, abilities, and gender.

1.3 Staff demonstrate prejudice against others (Ex. against child or other adult from different race or cultural group, against person with disability). *

3.1 Some racial and cultural diversity visible in materials (Ex. multi-racial or multi-cultural dolls, books, or bulletin board pictures, music tapes from many cultures; in bilingual areas some materials accessible in children's primary language). *

3.2 Materials show diversity (Ex. different races, cultures, ages, abilities, or gender) in a positive way. *

3.3 Staff intervene appropriately to counteract prejudice shown by children or other adults (Ex. discuss similarities and differences; establish rules for fair treatment of others), *or* no prejudice is shown.

5.1 Many books, pictures, and materials accessible showing people of different races, cultures, ages, abilities, and gender in non-stereotyping roles (Ex. both historical and current images; males and females shown doing many different types of work including traditional and non-traditional roles). *

5.2 Some props representing various cultures included for use in dramatic play (Ex. dolls of different races, ethnic clothing, cooking and eating utensils from various cultural groups). *

7.1 Inclusion of diversity is part of daily routines and play activities (Ex. ethnic foods are a regular part of meals/snacks; music tapes and songs from different cultures included at music time).

7.2 Activities included to promote understanding and acceptance of diversity (Ex. parents encouraged to share family customs with children; many cultures represented in holiday celebration).

(See Notes for Clarification and Questions on next page)

Item 28. When assessing diversity in materials, consider all areas and materials used by children, including pictures and photos displayed, books, puzzles, games, dolls, play people in the block area, puppets, music tapes, videos, and computer software.

1.3. Score "Yes" only if there is obvious, deliberate, and repeated prejudice shown. Do not score "Yes" if one isolated example of "politically incorrect" or "culturally insensitive behavior" is observed (e.g., teacher asks children to "sit Indian style"). However, in order to sensitize the staff, any such instance should be mentioned, for example in technical assistance associated with the scales.

3.1. "Some" means at least one example of racial diversity and at least one example of cultural diversity are present and easily seen by the children in the classroom used by the group most of the day.

3.2. If stereotyping or violence is shown with regard to any group, such as some "Cowboy and Indian" toys, then this indicator should be scored *No*. Gender equity should also be considered here. Portrayals of men/boys doing traditionally male activities and women/girls doing traditionally female activities are acceptable. However, do not give credit if gender stereotyping is portrayed negatively in any way. Look for problems that would be easily obvious to the children. It is not necessary to search avidly for negative examples. When historic cultural traditions are represented, the images must be balanced with non-traditional modern representations. For example, if traditional African tribal cultures are represented in materials, then current representations must also be included.

5.1. For this indicator, many books, many pictures, and many materials are required, and *all* categories of diversity listed need to be included to some degree. However, many examples of each category are not required. Materials must be located in spaces children use for a substantial portion of the day. Materials located in spaces used only for relatively short periods (e.g., hallways, entry way, lunch room, early AM or late PM classroom) are not counted to meet the requirements of this indicator.

5.2. To give credit, more than two examples must be observed to be accessible either indoors or outdoors, and obvious to the children. Examples include different kinds of dolls, puppets, and block/dramatic play people; dress-up clothes, foods, eating and cooking utensils from different cultures.

Questions

3.1. Could you give me examples of the types of music you use with the children?

3.3. What do you do if a child or adult shows prejudice?

7.2. Are any activities used to help children understand the variety of people in our country and in the world? Please give some examples.

Inadequate		Minimal		Good		Excellent
1	2	3	4	5	6	7

INTERACTION

29. Supervision of gross motor activities*

1.1 Inadequate supervision provided in gross motor area to protect children's health and safety (Ex. children left unattended even for short period of time; not enough adults to watch children in area; staff do not pay attention to children). *

1.2 Most staff-child interaction is negative (Ex. staff seem angry; punitive and overly controlling atmosphere). *

3.1 Supervision is adequate to protect children's health and safety (Ex. enough staff present to watch children in area; staff positioned to see all areas; staff move around as needed; intervene when problem occurs).

3.2 Some positive staff-child interaction (Ex. comfort child who is upset or hurt; show appreciation of new skill; pleasant tone of voice). *

5.1 Staff act to prevent dangerous situations before they occur (Ex. remove broken toys or other dangers prior to children's use; stop rough play before children get hurt).

5.2 Most staff-child interactions are pleasant and helpful. *

5.3 Staff assist children to develop skills needed to use equipment (Ex. help children learn to pump on swing; help child with disabilities use adaptive pedals on tricycle).

7.1 Staff talk with children about ideas related to their play (Ex. bring in concepts such as near-far, fast-slow for younger children; ask children to tell about building project or dramatic play).

7.2 Staff help with resources to enhance play (Ex. help set up obstacle course for tricycles).

7.3 Staff help children develop positive social interactions (Ex. help children to take turns on popular equipment; provide equipment that encourages cooperation such as a two-person rocking boat, walkie-talkie communication devices).

---

*Notes for Clarification

Item 29. To score this item, consider *all* teachers supervising gross motor activities and *all* children of similar age/abilities as those in the group you are observing. Notice whether adults are supervising the most hazardous areas/activities adequately.

1.1. The *example* in this indicator, of children being left unattended even for a short period of the time, means that *no* adult is present to supervise children.

1.2. "Most" means over 50% of all interactions during gross motor times, including both verbal and non-verbal.

3.2. "Some positive staff-child interaction" means that most exchanges are either neutral or positive, and at least two positive instances must be observed. To give credit, most interactions cannot be negative.

5.2. "Most staff-child interactions" means that the vast majority of verbal and non-verbal interactions are positive. Neutral interactions must be outweighed by positive and helpful interactions. There may be one or two slightly negative interactions but no extremely negative ones observed.

Questions

Could you describe how staff supervise children during gross motor activities and outdoor play?

5.3. What happens when children have difficulty using equipment?

Inadequate		Minimal		Good		Excellent
1	2	3	4	5	6	7

30. General supervision of children (other than gross motor)*

1.1 Inadequate supervision of children (Ex. staff leave children unsupervised; children's safety not protected; staff attend mainly to other tasks).

1.2 Most supervision is punitive or overly controlling (Ex. yelling, belittling children, constant "No's"). *

3.1 Sufficient supervision to protect children's safety.

3.2 Attention given to cleanliness and to prevent inappropriate use of materials (Ex. messy science table cleaned up; child stopped from emptying whole glue bottle).

3.3 Most supervision is non-punitive, and control is exercised in a reasonable way. *

5.1 Careful supervision of all children adjusted appropriately for different ages and abilities (Ex. Younger or more impulsive children supervised more closely).

5.2 Staff give children help and encouragement when needed (Ex. help child who is wandering get involved in play, help child complete puzzle).

5.3 Staff show awareness of the whole group even when working with one child or a small group (Ex. staff frequently scan room when working with one child, make sure area not visible is supervised by other staff).

5.4 Staff show appreciation of children's efforts and accomplishments.

7.1 Staff talk to children about ideas related to their play, asking questions and adding information to extend children's thinking.

7.2 A balance is maintained between the child's need to explore independently and staff input into learning (Ex. child allowed to complete painting before being asked to talk about it; child allowed to discover that her block building is unbalanced when it falls).

*Notes for Clarification

Item 30. The score for this item must be based on what is seen throughout the observation, during routines and play activities. Do not score until supervision has been observed under a wide range of circumstances, including more relaxed and more stressful times.

1.2, 3.3. "Most supervision" means the majority (over 50%) of supervision that has been observed.

Inadequate		Minimal		Good		Excellent
1	2	3	4	5	6	7

31. Discipline

1.1 Children are controlled with severe methods (Ex. spanking, shouting, confining children for long periods, or withholding food).

1.2 Discipline is so lax that there is little order or control.

1.3 Expectations for behavior are largely inappropriate for age and developmental level of children (Ex. everyone must be quiet at meals; children must wait quietly for long periods of time).

3.1 Staff do not use physical punishment or severe methods.

3.2 Staff usually maintain enough control to prevent children from hurting one another.

3.3 Expectations for behavior are largely appropriate for age and developmental level of children.

5.1 Staff use non-punitive discipline methods effectively (Ex. giving attention for positive behaviors; redirecting child from unacceptable to acceptable activity).

5.2 Program is set up to avoid conflict and promote age-appropriate interaction (Ex. duplicate toys accessible; child with favorite toy given protected place to play).

5.3 Staff react consistently to children's behavior (Ex. different staff apply same rules and use same methods; basic rules followed with all children). *

7.1 Staff actively involve children in solving their conflicts and problems (Ex. help children talk out problems and think of solutions; sensitize children to feelings of others).

7.2 Staff use activities to help children understand social skills (Ex. use storybooks and group discussions with children to work through common conflicts). *

7.3 Staff seek advice from other professionals concerning behavior problems. *

---

*Notes for Clarification

5.3. There needs to be general consistency among staff members in the way they handle different situations and children. This does not mean that there can be no flexibility. Basic rules for positive social interaction in a group, such as no hitting or hurting, respect for others and for materials, should always be followed. A specialized program may be needed to help a child with a disability follow basic classroom rules.

7.2. To give credit the activities must be done regularly enough to have an impact on the children's understanding—at least once a week.

7.3. In most cases "other professionals" means someone from outside the program that specializes in the area of concern. The early childhood professionals (teachers, director, etc.) who work in the classrooms and center can benefit from an outsider's perspective of a child who is experiencing difficulties. In a few cases, however, a program staff member can count as the "other professional" if the person has a specialization in the area of concern and can give an unbiased perspective.

Questions

1.1. Do you ever find it necessary to use strict discipline? Please describe the methods you use.

7.2. Do you use activities with the children that encourage them to get along well with each other? If so, please explain.

7.3. What do you do if you have a child with a very difficult behavior problem?

Inadequate		Minimal		Good		Excellent
1	2	3	4	5	6	7

32. Staff-child interactions*

1.1 Staff members are not responsive to or not involved with children (Ex. ignore children, staff seem distant or cold).

1.2 Interactions are unpleasant (Ex. voices sound strained and irritable). *

1.3 Physical contact used principally for control (Ex. hurrying children along) or inappropriately (Ex. unwanted hugs or tickling).

3.1 Staff usually respond to children in a warm, supportive manner (Ex. staff and children seem relaxed, voices cheerful, frequent smiling).

3.2 Few, if any, unpleasant interactions.

5.1 Staff show warmth through appropriate physical contact (Ex. pat child on the back, return child's hug).

5.2 Staff show respect for children (Ex. listen attentively, make eye contact, treat children fairly, do not discriminate).

5.3 Staff respond sympathetically to help children who are upset, hurt, or angry. *

7.1 Staff seem to enjoy being with the children.

7.2 Staff encourage the development of mutual respect between children and adults (Ex. staff wait until children finish asking questions before answering; encourage children in a polite way to listen when adults speak).

---

*Notes for Clarification

Item 32. While the indicators for quality in this item generally hold true across a diversity of cultures and individuals, the ways in which they are expressed may differ. For example, direct eye contact in some cultures is a sign of respect; in others, a sign of disrespect. Similarly, some individuals are more likely to smile and be demonstrative than others. However, the requirements of the indicators must be met, although there can be some variation in the way this is done.

1.2. Score this indicator "Yes" only if many unpleasant interactions are observed throughout the observation or during one part of the observation. If only one or two brief instances are observed, and most interactions are neutral or positive, score "No."

5.3. Sympathetic response means that staff notice and validate a child's feelings, even if the child is showing emotions that are often considered unacceptable, such as anger or impatience. The feelings should be accepted although inappropriate behaviors, such as hitting or throwing things, should not be allowed.

A sympathetic response should be provided in most, but not necessarily all, cases. If children are able to solve minor problems themselves, then a teacher response is not needed. The observer needs to get an overall impression of the response of the staff. If minor problems persist and are ignored or if staff respond in an unsympathetic manner, give no credit for this indicator.

Inadequate		Minimal		Good		Excellent
1	2	3	4	5	6	7

33. Interactions among children

1.1 Interaction among children (peers) not encouraged (Ex. talking with peers discouraged, few opportunities for children to choose own playmates).

1.2 Little or no staff guidance for positive peer interaction.

1.3 Little or no positive peer interaction (Ex. teasing, bickering, fighting are common).

3.1 Peer interaction encouraged (Ex. children allowed to move freely so natural groupings and interactions can occur).

3.2 Staff stop negative and hurtful peer interactions (Ex. stop name calling, fighting).

3.3 Some positive peer interaction occurs.

5.1 Staff model good social skills (Ex. are kind to others, listen, empathize, cooperate).

5.2 Staff help children develop appropriate social behavior with peers (Ex. help children talk through conflicts instead of fighting; encourage socially isolated children to find friends; help children understand feelings of others).

7.1 Peer interactions usually positive (Ex. older children often cooperate and share; children generally play well together without fighting).

7.2 Staff provide some opportunities for children to work together to complete a task (Ex. a group of children work to cover a large mural paper with many drawings; make a soup with many ingredients; cooperate to bring chairs to table).

Question

7.2. Are there any activities you use that encourage children to work together? Could you give me some examples?

Inadequate		Minimal		Good		Excellent
1	2	3	4	5	6	7

PROGRAM STRUCTURE

34. Schedule

1.1 Schedule is *either* too rigid, leaving no time for individual interests, *or* too flexible (chaotic), lacking a dependable sequence of daily events. *

3.1 Basic daily schedule exists that is familiar to children (Ex. routines and activities occur in relatively the same sequence most days).

3.2 Written schedule is posted in room and relates generally to what occurs. *

3.3 At least one indoor and one outdoor play period (weather permitting) occurs daily. *

3.4 Both gross motor and less active play occur daily.

5.1 Schedule provides balance of structure and flexibility (Ex. regularly scheduled outdoor play period may be lengthened in good weather).

5.2 A variety of play activities occur each day, some teacher directed and some child initiated.

5.3 A substantial portion of the day is used for play activities.

5.4 No long period of waiting during transitions between daily events. *

7.1 Smooth transitions between daily events (Ex. materials ready for next activity before current activity ends; most transitions handled a few children at a time rather than whole group).

7.2 Variations made in schedule to meet individual needs (Ex. shorter story time for child with short attention span; child working on project allowed to continue past scheduled time; slow eater may finish at own pace).

Notes for Clarification

1.1. "Daily events" refers to time for indoor and outdoor play activities as well as routines such as meals/snacks, nap/rest, and greeting/departing.

3.2. The "written schedule" need not be followed to the minute. The intent of this indicator is that the general sequence of events is being followed. The written schedule must be posted in the room to get credit; outside the door is not acceptable.

3.3. Both the indoor and outdoor play periods must each equal at least 1 hour in length for programs operating 8 hours or more (see "Explanation of Terms Used Throughout the Scale" on p. 7 for requirements for programs operating less than 8 hours a day).

5.4. "Long period of waiting" means waiting without any activity for three minutes or more *between daily events*, (e.g., running around aimlessly, whole group sitting at tables waiting for lunch, waiting in line to go out or to use the bathroom). Note that this indicator refers to waiting between transitions from one activity to another, rather than waiting within any activity.

Inadequate		Minimal		Good		Excellent
1	2	3	4	5	6	7

35. Free play*

1.1 *Either* little opportunity for free play *or* much of day spent in unsupervised free play.

1.2 Inadequate toys, games, and equipment provided for children to use in free play.

3.1 Some free play occurs daily indoors *and* outdoors, weather permitting. *

3.2 Supervision provided to protect children's health and safety. *

3.3 Some toys, games, and equipment accessible for children to use in free play.

5.1 Free play occurs for a substantial portion of the day both indoors and outdoors (Ex. several free play periods scheduled daily).

5.2 Supervision provided to facilitate children's play (Ex. staff help children get materials they need; help children use materials that are hard to manage).

5.3 Ample and varied toys, games, and equipment provided for free play.

7.1 Supervision used as an educational interaction (Ex. staff help children think through solutions to conflicts, encourage children to talk about activities, introduce concepts in relation to play).

7.2 New materials/experiences for free play added periodically (Ex. materials rotated; activities added in response to children's interests).

---

*Notes for Clarification

Item 35. Child is permitted to select materials and companions, and as far as possible manage play independently. Adult interaction is in response to child's needs. Situations in which children are assigned to centers by staff or staff select the materials that individual children may use do not count as free play.

3.1. "Free play" or free choice does not require that all areas are open for children's choice. The number of centers may be limited as long as the children may choose where, with what, and with whom they play. To give credit, children must be able to participate in free play for at least 1 hour daily in full-day programs of 8 hours or more. The 1 hour may take place at one time, or be a combination of times throughout the day (see "Explanation of Terms Used Throughout the Scale" on p. 7 for time required for programs operating less than 8 hours a day).

3.2. This indicator assesses whether children are supervised to minimize major hazards to their health and safety during free play, indoors and out, but does not apply to routines or other supervision (e.g., children are supervised so that they do not play with matches or swallow poisons, etc.). Do not score "No" unless supervision during free play is extremely lax.

Questions

Could you describe any free play opportunities the children might have? When and where do these occur? What can children play with?

Inadequate		Minimal		Good		Excellent
1	2	3	4	5	6	7

36. Group time

1.1 Children kept together as whole group most of the day (Ex. all do same art project, have story read to them, listen to records, use bathroom at the same time). *

1.2 Very few opportunities for staff to interact with individual children or small groups. *

3.1 Some play activities done in small groups or individually. *

3.2 Some opportunity for children to be a part of self-selected small groups. *

5.1 Whole-group gatherings limited to short periods, suited to age and individual needs of children. *

5.2 Many play activities done in small groups or individually. *

5.3 Some routines done in small groups or individually.

7.1 Different groupings provide a change of pace throughout the day.

7.2 Staff engage in educational interaction with small groups and individual children as well as with the whole group (Ex. read story, help small group with cooking or science activity). *

7.3 Many opportunities for children to be a part of self-selected small groups.

---

*Notes for Clarification

1.1. "Whole group" generally means all the children in the class. However, if a very large group is broken into two large groups, and the children in each group must participate in the same activity, consider this a whole-group time. "Kept together as whole group most of the day" means 75% of the time the children are in the program.

1.2, 3.1, 3.2, 5.2. The definition of small groups may change with the age and individual needs of the children. For typically developing 2- and 3-year-olds, a suitable small group might be three-to-five children, whereas for 4- and 5-year-olds, five-to-eight children might be manageable.

5.1. "Whole-group gatherings" may not be suitable for children under 3½ years of age or some children with special needs. If this is the case, no group gatherings are required for a 5, and credit should be given for this indicator. One way to determine whether the whole-group gathering is suitable is whether the children remain interested and involved.

5.2. To give credit for "many," at least half of the play activities observed should be completed in small groups or individually.

7.2. To give credit for this indicator, the assessor must observe to get a general impression of what the children experience. One staff member might be stronger in educational interaction than another, and if the stronger teacher is strong enough, credit can be given.

Inadequate		Minimal		Good		Excellent
1	2	3	4	5	6	7

37. Provisions for children with disabilities*

1.1 No attempt by staff to assess children's needs or find out about available assessments.

1.2 No attempt to meet children's special needs (Ex. needed modifications not made in teacher interaction, physical environment, program activities, schedule).

1.3 No involvement of parents in helping staff understand children's needs or in setting goals for the children.

1.4 Very little involvement of children with disabilities with the rest of the group (Ex. children do not eat at same table; wander and do not participate in activities).

3.1 Staff have information from available assessments.

3.2 Minor modifications made to meet the needs of children with disabilities. *

3.3 Some involvement of parents and classroom staff in setting goals (Ex. parents and teacher attend IEP or IFSP meeting).

3.4 Some involvement of children with disabilities in the ongoing activities with the other children.

5.1 Staff follow through with activities and interactions recommended by other professionals (Ex. medical doctors, educators) to help children meet identified goals.

5.2 Modifications made in environment, program, and schedule so that children can participate in many activities with others.

5.3 Parents frequently involved in sharing information with staff, setting goals, and giving feedback about how program is working.

7.1 Most of the professional intervention is carried out within the regular activities of the classroom.

7.2 Children with disabilities are integrated into the group and participate in most activities.

7.3 Staff contribute to individual assessments and intervention plans.

*Notes for Clarification

Item 37. Note that this item is scored only if there is a child in the group with an identified and diagnosed disability, with a completed assessment. If the diagnosis and assessment have not been completed on the child, (or if there is no child with a disability included in the classroom), score this item NA. If the child is receiving services, this can be accepted as evidence that a diagnosis and assessment exist. Existence of an IEP/IFSP is not required to score this item. To ensure privacy for families, the teacher need not point out the child or tell the observer about the particulars of the disability. As you question the teacher about how the identified child's special needs are handled, you do not need to know which child is being discussed.

3.2. "Minor modifications" may include limited changes in the environment (such as a ramp) to allow the children to attend, or a therapist who visits the program to work with the children periodically.

Questions

Could you describe how you try to meet the needs of the children with disabilities in your group?

1.1, 3.1. Do you have any information from assessments on the children? How is it used?

1.2, 3.2, 5.2. Do you need to do anything special to meet the needs of the children? Please describe what you do.

1.3, 3.3, 5.3. Are you and the children's parents involved in helping to decide how to meet the children's needs? Please describe.

5.1, 7.1. How are intervention services such as therapy handled?

7.3. Are you involved in the children's assessments or in the development of intervention plans? What is your role?

Inadequate		Minimal		Good		Excellent
1	2	3	4	5	6	7

PARENTS AND STAFF

38. Provisions for parents

1.1 No information concerning program given to parents in writing.

1.2 Parents discouraged from observing or being involved in children's program.

3.1 Parents given administrative information about program in writing (Ex. fees, hours of service, health rules for attendance).

3.2 Some sharing of child-related information between parents and staff (Ex. informal communication; parent conferences only upon request; some parenting materials).

3.3 Some possibilities for parents and family members to be involved in children's program.

3.4 Interactions between family members and staff are generally respectful and positive.

5.1 Parents urged to observe in child's group prior to enrollment.

5.2 Parents made aware of philosophy and approaches practiced (Ex. parent handbook, discipline policy, descriptions of activities).

5.3 Much sharing of child-related information between parents and staff (Ex. frequent informal communication; periodic conferences for all children; parent meetings, newsletters, parenting information available).

5.4 Variety of alternatives used to encourage family involvement in children's program. (Ex. bring birthday treat, eat lunch with child, attend family pot luck).

7.1 Parents asked for an evaluation of the program annually (Ex. parent questionnaires, group evaluation meetings).

7.2 Parents referred to other professionals when needed (Ex. for special parenting help, for health concerns about child).

7.3 Parents involved in decision making roles in program along with staff (Ex. parent representatives on board).

Questions

1.1, 3.1. Is any written information about the program given to parents? What is included in this information?

1.2, 3.3, 5.4. Are there any ways that parents can be involved in their child's classroom? Please give some examples.

3.2, 5.3. Do you and the parents ever share information about the children? How is this done?

3.4. What is your relationship with the parents usually like?

5.1. Are parents able to visit the class before their child is enrolled? How is this handled?

7.1. Do parents take part in evaluating the program? How is this done? About how often?

7.2. What do you do when parents seem to be having difficulties? Do you refer them to other professionals for help?

7.3. Do parents take part in making decisions about the program? How is this handled?

Inadequate		Minimal		Good		Excellent
1	2	3	4	5	6	7

39. Provisions for personal needs of staff

1.1 No special areas for staff (Ex. no separate restroom, lounge, storage for personal belongings).

1.2 No time provided away from children to meet personal needs (Ex. no time for breaks).

3.1 Separate adult restroom.

3.2 Some adult furniture available outside of children's play space.

3.3 Some storage for personal belongings.

3.4 Staff have at least one break daily.

3.5 Accommodation made to meet needs of staff with disabilities when necessary.
NA permitted.

5.1 Lounge with adult-sized furniture available; lounge may have dual use (Ex. office, conference room).

5.2 Convenient storage for personal belongings with security provisions when necessary. *

5.3 Morning, afternoon, and midday "lunch" breaks provided daily. *

5.4 Facilities provided for staff meals/snacks (Ex. refrigerator space, cooking facilities).

7.1 Separate adult lounge area (no dual use).

7.2 Comfortable adult furniture in lounge.

7.3 Staff have some flexibility in deciding when to take breaks.

---

*Notes for Clarification

5.2. Storage is considered "convenient" only if it does not require the staff to leave the classroom or neglect the care of the children to get their belongings.

5.3. These requirements are based on an 8-hour work day and should be adjusted for shorter periods. If teachers prefer to leave early, rather than taking breaks, then score this indicator "Yes."

Questions

1.2, 3.4, 5.3. Do you get time off during the day, when you can be away from the children? When does this happen?

3.3, 5.2. Where do you usually store your personal things, such as your coat or purse? How does this work out?

Inadequate		Minimal		Good		Excellent
1	2	3	4	5	6	7

40. Provisions for professional needs of staff

1.1 No access to phone. *

1.2 No file or storage space for staff materials (Ex. no space to keep materials staff need to prepare activities).

1.3 No space available for individual conferences during hours children are in attendance.

3.1 Convenient access to phone. *

3.2 Access to some file and storage space.

3.3 Some space available for individual conferences during hours children are in attendance.

5.1 Access to ample file and storage space.

5.2 Separate office space used for program administration. *

5.3 Space for conferences and adult group meetings is satisfactory (Ex. dual or shared use does not make scheduling difficult; privacy is assured; adult-sized furniture available).

7.1 Well-equipped office space for program administration (Ex. computer, answering machine used).

7.2 Program has space that can be used for individual conferences and group meetings that is conveniently located, comfortable, and separate from space used for children's activities.

*Notes for Clarification

1.1. The phone does not have to be located in the classroom, but it must be readily accessible. For example, if the phone is in another building, on another floor, or in a locked office, then this indicator is scored "Yes."

3.1. To give credit for this indicator, there must be a phone in the classroom for emergency calls or brief conversations with parents. A cell phone is acceptable if it is accessible.

5.2. The director's office in a child care center or the office in a public school are considered "separate office space." The office must be on-site to be given credit.

Questions

1.1, 3.1. Do you have access to a telephone? Where?

1.2, 3.2, 5.1. Do you have access to any file and storage space? Please describe.

1.3, 3.3, 5.3, 7.2. Is there any space you can use for parent/teacher conferences or for adult group meetings when the children are present? Please describe.

5.2, 7.1. Is there an office for the program? Please describe.

Inadequate		Minimal		Good		Excellent
1	2	3	4	5	6	7

41. Staff interaction and cooperation*

1.1 No communication among staff members of necessary information to meet children's needs (Ex. information regarding early departure of child is not communicated).

1.2 Interpersonal relationships interfere with caregiving responsibilities (Ex. staff socialize instead of looking after children or are curt and angry with one another).

1.3 Staff duties not shared fairly (Ex. one staff member handles most duties, while another is relatively uninvolved). *

3.1 Some basic information to meet children's needs is communicated (Ex. all staff know about child's allergies).

3.2 Interpersonal interaction among staff does not interfere with caregiving responsibilities.

3.3 Staff duties are shared fairly. *

5.1 Child-related information is communicated daily among staff (Ex. information about how routines and play activities are going for specific children).

5.2 Staff interactions are positive and add a feeling of warmth and support.

5.3 Responsibilities are shared so both care and play activities are handled smoothly. *

7.1 Staff working with the same group or in the same room have planning time together at least every other week.

7.2 Responsibilities of each staff member are clearly defined (Ex. one sets out play materials while the other greets children; one helps children prepare for rest, while the other supervises tooth-brushing). *

7.3 Program promotes positive interaction among staff members (Ex. by organizing social events; by encouraging group attendance at professional meetings).

Notes for Clarification

Item 41. Score if two or more staff members work with the group being observed, even if they work with the same group at different times. Score this item NA if there is only one staff member with group.

1.3, 3.3, 5.3, 7.2. "Staff duties shared fairly" means that all staff are busily involved on assigned tasks and the work gets done. (For further discussion of sharing of duties see *All About the ECERS-R*, p. 423.)

Questions

1.1, 3.1, 5.1. Do you have a chance to share information about the children with the other staff that work with your group? When and how often does this happen? What kinds of things do you talk about?

7.1. Do you have any planning time with your co-teacher(s)? About how often?

7.2. How do you and your co-teacher(s) decide what each of you will do?

7.3. Does the program ever organize events that you and other staff participate in together? Could you give me some examples?

Inadequate		Minimal		Good		Excellent
1	2	3	4	5	6	7

42. Supervision and evaluation of staff*

1.1 No supervision provided for staff.

1.2 No feedback or evaluation provided about staff performance.

3.1 Some supervision provided for staff (Ex. director observes informally; observation done in case of complaint).

3.2 Some feedback about performance provided.

5.1 Annual supervisory observation provided.

5.2 Written evaluation of performance shared with staff at least yearly.

5.3 Strengths of staff as well as areas needing improvement identified in the evaluation.

5.4 Action is taken to implement the recommendations of the evaluation (Ex. training given to improve performance; new materials purchased, if needed). *NA permitted.*

7.1 Staff participate in self-evaluation.

7.2 Frequent observations and feedback given to staff in addition to annual observation.

7.3 Feedback from supervision is given in a helpful, supportive manner.

---

*Notes for Clarification

Item 42. Score this item NA only when the program is a one-person operation, with no other staff. Get information to score this item from the person being supervised, not from the supervisor, except in cases where classroom staff state that they do not know. Then ask the supervisor.

Questions

1.1, 3.1, 5.1, 5.2. Is your work supervised in any way? How is this done?

1.2, 3.2, 5.2, 7.3. Are you ever given any feedback about your performance? How is this handled? How often?

5.4. If improvement is needed, how is this handled?

7.1. Do you ever take part in self-evaluation?

Inadequate		Minimal		Good		Excellent
1	2	3	4	5	6	7

43. Opportunities for professional growth*

1.1 No orientation to program or in-service training provided for staff.

1.2 No staff meetings held.

3.1 Some orientation for new staff including emergency, safety, and health procedures. *

3.2 Some in-service training provided. *

3.3 Some staff meetings held to handle administrative concerns. *

5.1 Thorough orientation for new staff including interaction with children and parents, discipline methods, appropriate activities.

5.2 In-service training provided regularly by program (Ex. staff participate in workshops; guest speakers and videos used for on-site training). *

5.3 Monthly staff meetings held that include staff development activities.

5.4 Some professional resource materials available on-site (Ex. books, magazines, or other materials on child development, cultural sensitivity, and classroom activities—may be borrowed from library). *

7.1 Support available for staff to attend courses, conferences, or workshops not provided by the program (Ex. released time, travel costs, conference fees).

7.2 Good professional library containing current materials on a variety of early childhood subjects available on premises. *

7.3 Staff with less than an AA degree in early childhood education are required to continue formal education (Ex. work towards GED, CDA, AA).
NA permitted.

(See Notes for Clarification and Questions on next page)

*Notes for Clarification

Item 43. Get information to score this item from the classroom staff, unless the staff state that they do not know. Then ask the supervisor.

3.1. Basic orientation must take place within 6 weeks after the start of employment and include emergency, health, and safety procedures, in order to give credit.

3.2. In-service training, which all classroom staff are required to attend, must be provided at least once a year in order to give credit.

3.3. Staff meetings, which all classroom staff are expected to attend, must be held at least two times a year by the director and/or administrative staff in order to get credit.

5.2. In-service training, which all classroom staff are required to attend, must be provided at least two times a year, either on-site or in community workshops.

5.4. "Some" means that at least 25 books, pamphlets, or AV materials in good condition are available to staff.

7.2. "Current materials" are books that have been published within the last 10 years, and journals and magazines from the past 2 years. Books, such as the works of Piaget and Erikson, are exceptions, since they are classics on which many of our current ideas are based.

Questions

1.1, 3.1, 3.2, 5.1, 5.2. Is any training provided to staff? Please describe this training. What is done with new staff?

1.2, 3.3, 5.3. Do you ever have staff meetings? About how often? What is usually handled at these meetings?

5.4, 7.2. Are there any resources on-site that you can use for new ideas? What is included?

7.1. Is there any support provided so you can attend conferences or courses? Please describe what is available.

7.3. Are there any requirements for staff with less than an AA degree to continue their formal education? Please describe the requirements.

Sample of a Filled-in Score Sheet and Profile

Sample Score Sheet: Observation 1 9/18/97

LANGUAGE-REASONING *9/18/97*

15. Books & pictures   1 2 ③ 4 5 6 7   Notes:

Y N	Y N	Y N	Y N
1.1 ☐ ☑	3.1 ☑ ☐	5.1 ☐ ☑	7.1 ☐ ☐
1.2 ☐ ☑	3.2 ☑ ☐	5.2 ☑ ☐	7.2 ☐ ☐
		5.3 ☐ ☑	
		5.4 ☑ ☐	
		5.5 ☐ ☑	

- few books accessible
- one group storytime daily

16. Encouraging children to communicate   1 2 3 ④ 5 6 7

Y N	Y N	Y N	Y N
1.1 ☐ ☑	3.1 ☑ ☐	5.1 ☐ ☑	7.1 ☐ ☑
1.2 ☐ ☑	3.2 ☑ ☐	5.2 ☑ ☐	7.2 ☐ ☐
	3.3 ☑ ☐		

- communication materials accessible
- little staff involvement

17. Using language to develop reasoning skills   1 ② 3 4 5 6 7

Y N	Y N	Y N	Y N
1.1 ☐ ☑	3.1 ☑ ☐	5.1 ☐ ☐	7.1 ☐ ☐
1.2 ☐ ☑	3.2 ☐ ☑	5.2 ☐ ☐	7.2 ☐ ☐

- no instances observed of staff introducing logical reasoning concepts

18. Informal use of language   1 2 ③ 4 5 6 7

Y N	Y N	Y N	Y N
1.1 ☐ ☑	3.1 ☑ ☐	5.1 ☐ ☑	7.1 ☐ ☐
1.2 ☐ ☑	3.2 ☑ ☐	5.2 ☐ ☑	7.2 ☐ ☐
1.3 ☐ ☑		5.3 ☐ ☑	
		5.4 ☐ ☑	

- frequent child-child conversations
- little staff-child conversation

A. Subscale (Items 15 - 18) Score *12*
B. Number of items scored *04*

LANGUAGE-REASONING Average Score (A ÷ B) *3.00*

Sample Score Sheet: Observation 2 4/29/98

LANGUAGE-REASONING *4/29/98*

15. Books & pictures   1 2 3 ④ 5 6 7   Notes:

Y N	Y N	Y N	Y N
1.1 ☐ ☑	3.1 ☑ ☐	5.1 ☐ ☑	7.1 ☐ ☐
1.2 ☑ ☐	3.2 ☑ ☐	5.2 ☑ ☐	7.2 ☐ ☐
		5.3 ☑ ☐	
		5.4 ☑ ☐	
		5.5 ☐ ☑	

- few books -
- no multi-cultural
- good center for reading and language materials
- flannel board used

16. Encouraging children to communicate   1 2 3 4 5 ⑥ 7

Y N	Y N	Y N	Y N
1.1 ☐ ☑	3.1 ☑ ☐	5.1 ☑ ☐	7.1 ☑ ☐
1.2 ☐ ☑	3.2 ☑ ☐	5.2 ☑ ☐	7.2 ☐ ☑
	3.3 ☑ ☐		

- no tie in with written language

17. Using language to develop reasoning skills   1 2 3 ④ 5 6 7

Y N	Y N	Y N	Y N
1.1 ☐ ☑	3.1 ☑ ☐	5.1 ☑ ☐	7.1 ☐ ☐
1.2 ☐ ☑	3.2 ☑ ☐	5.2 ☐ ☑	7.2 ☐ ☐

- reasoning games used only in free play -
- no staff feedback or input seen

18. Informal use of language   1 2 3 4 ⑤ 6 7

Y N	Y N	Y N	Y N
1.1 ☑ ☐	3.1 ☑ ☐	5.1 ☑ ☐	7.1 ☐ ☑
1.2 ☑ ☐	3.2 ☑ ☐	5.2 ☑ ☐	7.2 ☐ ☑
1.3 ☑ ☐		5.3 ☑ ☐	
		5.4 ☑ ☐	

staff conversation was only a few children
- no use of questions to get longer answers

A. Subscale (Items 15 - 18) Score *19*
B. Number of items scored *04*

LANGUAGE-REASONING Average Score (A ÷ B) *4.75*

Sample of a Profile

III. Language-Reasoning (15-18)

Obs. 1	Obs. 2
3	4.75

average subscale score

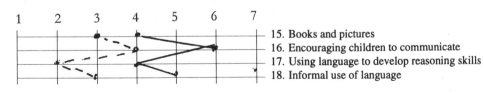

15. Books and pictures
16. Encouraging children to communicate
17. Using language to develop reasoning skills
18. Informal use of language

SCORE SHEET – EXPANDED VERSION
Early Childhood Environment Rating Scale–Revised
Thelma Harms, Richard M. Clifford, and Debby Cryer

Observer: _____

Center/School: _____

Room: _____

Teacher(s): _____

Observer Code: ___ ___ ___

Center Code: ___ ___ ___

Room Code: ___ ___

Teacher Code: ___ ___

Date of Observation: __ __ / __ __ / __ __
                    m m   d d   y y

Number of children with identified disabilities: ___ ___

Check type(s) of disability: ☐ physical/sensory ☐ cognitive/language ☐ social/emotional ☐ other: _____

Birthdates of children enrolled: youngest __ __ / __ __ / __ .
                                  m m d d y y

                        oldest __ __ / __ __ / __ __
                                m m d d y y

Time observation began: ___ ___ : ___ ___ ☐ AM ☐ PM

Time observation ended: ___ ___ : ___ ___ ☐ AM ☐ PM

Time interview began: ___ ___ : ___ ___ ☐ AM ☐ PM

Time interview ended: ___ ___ : ___ ___ ☐ AM ☐ PM

Time				
# of staff present				
# of children present				

Highest number center allows in class at one time: ___ ___

Highest number of children present during observation: ___ ___

SPACE AND FURNISHINGS

1. Indoor space

| 1 2 3 4 5 6 7 |

Y N	Y N NA	Y N	Y N
1.1 ☐ ☐	3.1 ☐ ☐	5.1 ☐ ☐	7.1 ☐ ☐
1.2 ☐ ☐	3.2 ☐ ☐	5.2 ☐ ☐	7.2 ☐ ☐
1.3 ☐ ☐	3.3 ☐ ☐	5.3 ☐ ☐	
1.4 ☐ ☐	3.4 ☐ ☐		
	3.5 ☐ ☐ ☐		

2. Furniture for care, play, & learning

| 1 2 3 4 5 6 7 |

Y N	Y N NA	Y N NA	Y N
1.1 ☐ ☐	3.1 ☐ ☐	5.1 ☐ ☐	7.1 ☐ ☐
1.2 ☐ ☐	3.2 ☐ ☐	5.2 ☐ ☐	7.2 ☐ ☐
	3.3 ☐ ☐ ☐	5.3 ☐ ☐ ☐	

5.1 Child-sized? _____ ÷ _____ = _____
               (# child-sized) (# children) (% child-sized)

3. Furnishings for relaxation

| 1 | 2 | 3 | 4 | 5 | 6 | 7 |

	Y	N		Y	N			Y	N		Y	N
1.1	☐	☐	3.1	☐	☐	S 5.1	☐	☐	7.1	☐	☐
1.2	☐	☐	3.2	☐	☐	5.2	☐	☐	7.2	☐	☐
						5.3	☐	☐			

5.1 Total time, cozy area: _____

S = substantial portion of the day

4. Room arrangement

| 1 | 2 | 3 | 4 | 5 | 6 | 7 |

	Y	N		Y	N	NA		Y	N		Y	N
1.1	☐	☐	3.1	☐	☐		5.1	☐	☐	7.1	☐	☐
1.2	☐	☐	3.2	☐	☐		5.2	☐	☐	7.2	☐	☐
			3.3	☐	☐		5.3	☐	☐	7.3	☐	☐
			3.4	☐	☐	☐						

3.1, 5.1, 7.1 List defined interest centers:

5. Space for privacy

| 1 | 2 | 3 | 4 | 5 | 6 | 7 |

	Y	N		Y	N			Y	N		Y	N
1.1	☐	☐	3.1	☐	☐	5.1	☐	☐	7.1	☐	☐
			3.2	☐	☐	S 5.2	☐	☐	7.2	☐	☐

5.2 Total time, space for privacy: _____

S = substantial portion of the day

6. Child-related display

| 1 | 2 | 3 | 4 | 5 | 6 | 7 |

	Y	N		Y	N			Y	N		Y	N
1.1	☐	☐	3.1	☐	☐	5.1	☐	☐	7.1	☐	☐
1.2	☐	☐	3.2	☐	☐	5.2	☐	☐	7.2	☐	☐
						5.3	☐	☐			

7. Space for gross motor

| 1 | 2 | 3 | 4 | 5 | 6 | 7 |

	Y	N		Y	N		Y	N		Y	N
1.1	☐	☐	3.1	☐	☐	5.1	☐	☐	7.1	☐	☐
1.2	☐	☐	3.2	☐	☐	5.2	☐	☐	7.2	☐	☐
						5.3	☐	☐	7.3	☐	☐

1.2, 3.2 Safety hazards:

	major	minor
outdoors		
indoors		

8. Gross motor equipment

| 1 2 3 4 5 6 7 |

	Y N		Y N		Y N NA		Y N
1.1	☐ ☐	3.1	☐ ☐	5.1	☐ ☐	7.1	☐ ☐
1.2	☐ ☐	3.2	☐ ☐	5.2	☐ ☐	7.2	☐ ☐
1.3	☐ ☐	3.3	☐ ☐	5.3	☐ ☐ ☐		

3.1 Total time, gross motor equipment: _____   7.1 stationary:

5.2 List variety of skills:
1)   5)
2)   6)   portable:
3)   7)
4)   8)

A. Total Subscale (Items 1–8) Score __ __   B. Number of items scored __ __   **SPACE AND FURNISHINGS** Average Score (A ÷ B) __.__ __

PERSONAL CARE ROUTINES

9. Greeting/departing

| 1 2 3 4 5 6 7 |

	Y N		Y N		Y N NA		Y N NA
1.1	☐ ☐	3.1	☐ ☐	5.1	☐ ☐	7.1	☐ ☐
1.2	☐ ☐	3.2	☐ ☐	5.2	☐ ☐	7.2	☐ ☐
1.3	☐ ☐	3.3	☐ ☐	5.3	☐ ☐ ☐	7.3	☐ ☐ ☐

1.1, 3.1, 5.1, 5.3, 7.3 Greetings observed (✓=yes, ✗=no)

	Child	Parent	Info shared
1	____	____	____
2	____	____	____
3	____	____	____
4	____	____	____
5	____	____	____
6	____	____	____

10. Meals/snacks

| 1 2 3 4 5 6 7 |

	Y N NA		Y N NA		Y N NA		Y N
1.1	☐ ☐	3.1	☐ ☐	5.1	☐ ☐	7.1	☐ ☐
1.2	☐ ☐	3.2	☐ ☐	5.2	☐ ☐	7.2	☐ ☐
1.3	☐ ☐	3.3	☐ ☐	5.3	☐ ☐	7.3	☐ ☐
1.4	☐ ☐	3.4	☐ ☐	5.4	☐ ☐ ☐		
1.5	☐ ☐ ☐	3.5	☐ ☐ ☐				
		3.6	☐ ☐ ☐				

1.3, 3.3 Sanitary conditions observed (✓=yes, ✗=no)

	1	2	3	4	5	6	7	8	9	10	11	12	13	14	15
Children's hands washed															
Teachers' hands washed															

Tables sanitized?

Other problems?

11. Nap/rest

| 1 2 3 4 5 6 7 NA |

	Y N		Y N		Y N		Y N
1.1	☐ ☐	3.1	☐ ☐	5.1	☐ ☐	7.1	☐ ☐
1.2	☐ ☐	3.2	☐ ☐	5.2	☐ ☐	7.2	☐ ☐
1.3	☐ ☐	3.3	☐ ☐	5.3	☐ ☐		
		3.4	☐ ☐				

	Y N
3.2 All cots/mats ≥ 18" apart?	☐ ☐
5.3 All cots/mats ≥ 36" apart?	☐ ☐

12. Toileting/diapering

| 1 | 2 | 3 | 4 | 5 | 6 | 7 |

	Y	N		Y	N		Y	N		Y	N
1.1	☐	☐	3.1	☐	☐	5.1	☐	☐	7.1	☐	☐
1.2	☐	☐	3.2	☐	☐	5.2	☐	☐	7.2	☐	☐
1.3	☐	☐	3.3	☐	☐	5.3	☐	☐			
1.4	☐	☐	3.4	☐	☐						
			3.5	☐	☐						

1.3, 3.3 Handwashing observed (✓=yes, ✗=no)

	1	2	3	4	5	6	7	8	9	10	11	12	13	14	15
Child															
Teacher															

Adult handwashing completed ____ out of ____ times

Percentage completed = ____ %

Child handwashing completed ____ out of ____ times

Percentage completed = ____ %

3.1 Sanitary conditions (✓=yes, ✗=no)

Toilets flushed? ____   Same sink sanitized? ____

Other issues:

13. Health practices

| 1 | 2 | 3 | 4 | 5 | 6 | 7 |

	Y	N		Y	N		Y	N		Y	N	NA
1.1	☐	☐	3.1	☐	☐	5.1	☐	☐	7.1	☐	☐	
1.2	☐	☐	3.2	☐	☐	5.2	☐	☐	7.2	☐	☐	☐
			3.3	☐	☐	5.3	☐	☐				
			3.4	☐	☐							

1.1, 3.1, 3.2 Handwashing observations (tally)

	Adult		Child	
	Yes	No	Yes	No
Upon arrival in class or re-entry from outdoors				
After sand or messy play				
Before/after water play				
After dealing w/ bodily fluids				
After touching pets or contaminated objects				

Adult handwashing

Completed ____ out of ____ times

Percentage completed = ____ %

Child handwashing

Completed ____ out of ____ times

Percentage completed = ____ %

14. Safety practices

| 1 | 2 | 3 | 4 | 5 | 6 | 7 |

	Y	N		Y	N		Y	N		Y	N
1.1	☐	☐	3.1	☐	☐	5.1	☐	☐	7.1	☐	☐
1.2	☐	☐	3.2	☐	☐	5.2	☐	☐	7.2	☐	☐
1.3	☐	☐	3.3	☐	☐						

1.1, 3.1 Safety hazards:

	major	minor
outdoors		
indoors		

A. Total Subscale (Items 9–14) Score __ __   B. Number of items scored __ __   **PERSONAL CARE ROUTINES** Average Score (A ÷ B) __.__ __

LANGUAGE-REASONING

15. Books and pictures

| 1 | 2 | 3 | 4 | 5 | 6 | 7 |

	Y	N		Y	N			Y	N		Y	N
1.1	☐	☐	3.1	☐	☐	S	5.1	☐	☐	7.1	☐	☐
1.2	☐	☐	3.2	☐	☐		5.2	☐	☐	7.2	☐	☐
							5.3	☐	☐			
							5.4	☐	☐			
							5.5	☐	☐			

S = substantial portion of the day

5.1 Total time, books and pictures = _____

5.1 Wide selection (tally):   fantasy _____

nature/science _____   factual _____   race/culture _____

people _____   abilities _____   animals _____

5.4 Violence? _____

Also see Item 26, 3.1 and 5.1, and Item 28, 3.1 and 5.1.

5.5 Informal reading observed? {y / n}

16. Encouraging children to communicate

1	2	3	4	5	6	7

	Y N		Y N		Y N		Y N
1.1	☐ ☐	3.1	☐ ☐	5.1	☐ ☐	7.1	☐ ☐
1.2	☐ ☐	3.2	☐ ☐	5.2	☐ ☐	7.2	☐ ☐
		3.3	☐ ☐				

5.1 Communication activities:
Examples during free play:

Examples during group time:

7.2 Examples of written communication:

17. Using language to develop reasoning skills

1	2	3	4	5	6	7

	Y N		Y N		Y N		Y N
1.1	☐ ☐	3.1	☐ ☐	5.1	☐ ☐	7.1	☐ ☐
1.2	☐ ☐	3.2	☐ ☐	5.2	☐ ☐	7.2	☐ ☐

3.1, 5.1 Examples of logical relationships:

5.2 Examples of child's explanations:

18. Informal use of language

1	2	3	4	5	6	7

	Y N		Y N		Y N		Y N
1.1	☐ ☐	3.1	☐ ☐	5.1	☐ ☐	7.1	☐ ☐
1.2	☐ ☐	3.2	☐ ☐	5.2	☐ ☐	7.2	☐ ☐
1.3	☐ ☐			5.3	☐ ☐		
				5.4	☐ ☐		

5.3 Examples of staff expanding on children's ideas:

7.2 Examples of staff questioning for longer answers:

A. Total Subscale (Items 15–18) Score __ __   B. Number of items scored __ __   LANGUAGE-REASONING Average Score (A ÷ B) __.__ __

ACTIVITIES

19. Fine motor

1	2	3	4	5	6	7

	Y N		Y N			Y N		Y N
1.1	☐ ☐	3.1	☐ ☐	S 5.1	☐ ☐	7.1	☐ ☐
1.2	☐ ☐	3.2	☐ ☐	5.2	☐ ☐	7.2	☐ ☐
				5.3	☐ ☐		

S = substantial portion of the day

5.1 Total time, fine motor activities: _____
5.1 Types of fine motor material (list 3 to 5 of each):

• Small building materials _____

• Art _____

• Manipulatives _____

• Puzzles _____

20. Art

1	2	3	4	5	6	7

	Y N		Y N		Y N		Y N NA
1.1 ☐ ☐		3.1 ☐ ☐	S 5.1 ☐ ☐		7.1 ☐ ☐
1.2 ☐ ☐		3.2 ☐ ☐	5.2 ☐ ☐		7.2 ☐ ☐
				7.3 ☐ ☐ ☐

S = substantial portion of the day

5.1 Total time, art materials: _____
5.1 Types of art materials (list 3 to 5 of each):

- **drawing** (required) _____
- paints _____
- 3-D _____
- collage _____   • tools _____

---

21. Music/movement

1	2	3	4	5	6	7

	Y N		Y N		Y N		Y N
1.1 ☐ ☐	3.1 ☐ ☐	5.1 ☐ ☐	7.1 ☐ ☐
1.2 ☐ ☐	3.2 ☐ ☐	5.2 ☐ ☐	7.2 ☐ ☐
	3.3 ☐ ☐		7.3 ☐ ☐

3.1, 5.1 Total time, music materials: _____
5.1 Types of music materials:

- instruments _____
- music to listen to, and for older children to play _____
- dance props with music _____

7.1 Music available as a free choice? _____   As a group activity? _____

---

22. Blocks

1	2	3	4	5	6	7

	Y N		Y N		Y N		Y N
1.1 ☐ ☐	3.1 ☐ ☐	5.1 ☐ ☐	7.1 ☐ ☐
	3.2 ☐ ☐	5.2 ☐ ☐	7.2 ☐ ☐
	3.3 ☐ ☐	5.3 ☐ ☐	7.3 ☐ ☐
		S 5.4 ☐ ☐

S = substantial portion of the day

5.4 Total time, block area: _____
7.1 Types of blocks (✓ =observed):
___ unit
___ large hollow
___ homemade
___ other: _____

---

23. Sand/water

1	2	3	4	5	6	7

	Y N		Y N		Y N		Y N
1.1 ☐ ☐	3.1 ☐ ☐	5.1 ☐ ☐	7.1 ☐ ☐
1.2 ☐ ☐	3.2 ☐ ☐	5.2 ☐ ☐	7.2 ☐ ☐
		5.3 ☐ ☐

3.1, 5.1, 7.1 Provision for… (✓ =observed):

	Indoors	Outdoors
Sand		
Water		

5.3 Total time, sand or water play: _____

---

24. Dramatic play

1	2	3	4	5	6	7

	Y N		Y N		Y N		Y N
1.1 ☐ ☐	3.1 ☐ ☐	5.1 ☐ ☐	7.1 ☐ ☐
	3.2 ☐ ☐	S 5.2 ☐ ☐	7.2 ☐ ☐
	3.3 ☐ ☐	5.3 ☐ ☐	7.3 ☐ ☐
		5.4 ☐ ☐	7.4 ☐ ☐

S = substantial portion of the day

5.1 Gender-specific dress-up clothing (list):

	Male	Female
1.		
2.		
3.		

5.3 Themes represented in props (name at least two):

5.2 Total time, dramatic play: _____

25. Nature/science

| 1 | 2 | 3 | 4 | 5 | 6 | 7 |

	Y N		Y N		Y N		Y N
1.1	☐ ☐	3.1	☐ ☐	5.1	☐ ☐	7.1	☐ ☐
		3.2	☐ ☐	S 5.2	☐ ☐	7.2	☐ ☐
		3.3	☐ ☐	5.3	☐ ☐		
				5.4	☐ ☐		

S = substantial portion of the day

5.1 Types of nature/science materials (list 3 to 5 of each):

- Collections of natural objects _____
- Living things _____
- Books, games, toys _____
- Activities _____

5.2 Total time, nature/science: _____

26. Math/number

| 1 | 2 | 3 | 4 | 5 | 6 | 7 |

	Y N		Y N		Y N		Y N
1.1	☐ ☐	3.1	☐ ☐	5.1	☐ ☐	7.1	☐ ☐
1.2	☐ ☐	3.2	☐ ☐	S 5.2	☐ ☐	7.2	☐ ☐
				5.3	☐ ☐		
				5.4	☐ ☐		

S = substantial portion of the day

5.1 Types of math/number materials (list 3 to 5 of each):

- Counting _____
- Written numbers _____
- Measuring _____
- Comparing quantities _____
- Shapes _____

5.2 Total time, math/number: _____

27. Use of TV, video, and/or computers

| 1 | 2 | 3 | 4 | 5 | 6 | 7 | NA |

	Y N		Y N		Y N NA		Y N NA
1.1	☐ ☐	3.1	☐ ☐	5.1	☐ ☐	7.1	☐ ☐ ☐
1.2	☐ ☐	3.2	☐ ☐	5.2	☐ ☐ ☐	7.2	☐ ☐
		3.3	☐ ☐	5.3	☐ ☐		
				5.4	☐ ☐		

28. Promoting acceptance of diversity

| 1 | 2 | 3 | 4 | 5 | 6 | 7 |

	Y N		Y N		Y N		Y N
1.1	☐ ☐	3.1	☐ ☐	5.1	☐ ☐	7.1	☐ ☐
1.2	☐ ☐	3.2	☐ ☐	5.2	☐ ☐	7.2	☐ ☐
1.3	☐ ☐	3.3	☐ ☐				

5.1 Diversity in materials (tally)

	Books	Pictures	Other materials
Races			
Cultures			
Ages			
Abilities			
Gender			

A. Total Subscale (Items 19–28) Score __ __   B. Number of items scored __ __   **ACTIVITIES Average Score (A ÷ B)** __.__ __

INTERACTION

29. Supervision of gross motor activities

| 1 2 3 4 5 6 7 |

	Y N		Y N		Y N		Y N
1.1	☐ ☐	3.1	☐ ☐	5.1	☐ ☐	7.1	☐ ☐
1.2	☐ ☐	3.2	☐ ☐	5.2	☐ ☐	7.2	☐ ☐
				5.3	☐ ☐	7.3	☐ ☐

30. General supervision of children

| 1 2 3 4 5 6 7 |

	Y N		Y N		Y N		Y N
1.1	☐ ☐	3.1	☐ ☐	5.1	☐ ☐	7.1	☐ ☐
1.2	☐ ☐	3.2	☐ ☐	5.2	☐ ☐	7.2	☐ ☐
		3.3	☐ ☐	5.3	☐ ☐		
				5.4	☐ ☐		

31. Discipline

| 1 2 3 4 5 6 7 |

	Y N		Y N		Y N		Y N
1.1	☐ ☐	3.1	☐ ☐	5.1	☐ ☐	7.1	☐ ☐
1.2	☐ ☐	3.2	☐ ☐	5.2	☐ ☐	7.2	☐ ☐
1.3	☐ ☐	3.3	☐ ☐	5.3	☐ ☐	7.3	☐ ☐

32. Staff-child interactions

| 1 2 3 4 5 6 7 |

	Y N		Y N		Y N		Y N
1.1	☐ ☐	3.1	☐ ☐	5.1	☐ ☐	7.1	☐ ☐
1.2	☐ ☐	3.2	☐ ☐	5.2	☐ ☐	7.2	☐ ☐
1.3	☐ ☐			5.3	☐ ☐		

33. Interactions among children

| 1 2 3 4 5 6 7 |

	Y N		Y N		Y N		Y N
1.1	☐ ☐	3.1	☐ ☐	5.1	☐ ☐	7.1	☐ ☐
1.2	☐ ☐	3.2	☐ ☐	5.2	☐ ☐	7.2	☐ ☐
1.3	☐ ☐	3.3	☐ ☐				

A. Total Subscale (Items 29–33) Score __ __   B. Number of items scored __ __   INTERACTION Average Score (A ÷ B) __.__ __

PROGRAM STRUCTURE

34. Schedule

| 1 2 3 4 5 6 7 |

	Y N		Y N		Y N		Y N
1.1	☐ ☐	3.1	☐ ☐	5.1	☐ ☐	7.1	☐ ☐
		3.2	☐ ☐	5.2	☐ ☐	7.2	☐ ☐
		3.3	☐ ☐	S 5.3	☐ ☐		
		3.4	☐ ☐	5.4	☐ ☐		

5.3 Time, indoor play: _____

Time, outdoor play: _____

Total time, play: _____

S = substantial portion of the day

35. Free play

| 1 2 3 4 5 6 7 |

	Y N		Y N		Y N		Y N
1.1	☐ ☐	3.1	☐ ☐	S 5.1	☐ ☐	7.1	☐ ☐
1.2	☐ ☐	3.2	☐ ☐	5.2	☐ ☐	7.2	☐ ☐
		3.3	☐ ☐	5.3	☐ ☐		

5.1 Time, free play indoors: _____

Time, free play outdoors: _____

Total time, free play: _____

S = substantial portion of the day

36. Group time

| 1 2 3 4 5 6 7 |

	Y N		Y N		Y N		Y N
1.1	☐ ☐	3.1	☐ ☐	5.1	☐ ☐	7.1	☐ ☐
1.2	☐ ☐	3.2	☐ ☐	5.2	☐ ☐	7.2	☐ ☐
				5.3	☐ ☐	7.3	☐ ☐

37. Provisions for children with disabilities

| 1 2 3 4 5 6 7 NA |

	Y N		Y N		Y N		Y N
1.1	☐ ☐	3.1	☐ ☐	5.1	☐ ☐	7.1	☐ ☐
1.2	☐ ☐	3.2	☐ ☐	5.2	☐ ☐	7.2	☐ ☐
1.3	☐ ☐	3.3	☐ ☐	5.3	☐ ☐	7.3	☐ ☐
1.4	☐ ☐	3.4	☐ ☐				

A. Total Subscale (Items 34–37) Score ___ ___   B. Number of items scored ___ ___   **PROGRAM STRUCTURE Average Score (A ÷ B)** ___.___ ___

PARENTS AND STAFF

38. Provisions for parents

| 1 2 3 4 5 6 7 |

	Y N		Y N		Y N		Y N
1.1	☐ ☐	3.1	☐ ☐	5.1	☐ ☐	7.1	☐ ☐
1.2	☐ ☐	3.2	☐ ☐	5.2	☐ ☐	7.2	☐ ☐
		3.3	☐ ☐	5.3	☐ ☐	7.3	☐ ☐
		3.4	☐ ☐	5.4	☐ ☐		

39. Provisions for personal needs of staff

| 1 2 3 4 5 6 7 |

	Y N		Y N NA		Y N		Y N
1.1	☐ ☐	3.1	☐ ☐	5.1	☐ ☐	7.1	☐ ☐
1.2	☐ ☐	3.2	☐ ☐	5.2	☐ ☐	7.2	☐ ☐
		3.3	☐ ☐	5.3	☐ ☐	7.3	☐ ☐
		3.4	☐ ☐	5.4	☐ ☐		
		3.5	☐ ☐ ☐				

40. Provisions for professional needs of staff

| 1 2 3 4 5 6 7 |

	Y N		Y N		Y N		Y N
1.1	☐ ☐	3.1	☐ ☐	5.1	☐ ☐	7.1	☐ ☐
1.2	☐ ☐	3.2	☐ ☐	5.2	☐ ☐	7.2	☐ ☐
1.3	☐ ☐	3.3	☐ ☐	5.3	☐ ☐		

41. Staff interaction and cooperation

| 1 2 3 4 5 6 7 NA |

	Y N		Y N		Y N		Y N
1.1	☐ ☐	3.1	☐ ☐	5.1	☐ ☐	7.1	☐ ☐
1.2	☐ ☐	3.2	☐ ☐	5.2	☐ ☐	7.2	☐ ☐
1.3	☐ ☐	3.3	☐ ☐	5.3	☐ ☐	7.3	☐ ☐

42. Supervision and evaluation of staff

| 1 2 3 4 5 6 7 NA |

	Y N		Y N		Y N NA		Y N
1.1	☐ ☐	3.1	☐ ☐	5.1	☐ ☐	7.1	☐ ☐
1.2	☐ ☐	3.2	☐ ☐	5.2	☐ ☐	7.2	☐ ☐
				5.3	☐ ☐	7.3	☐ ☐
				5.4	☐ ☐ ☐		

43. Opportunities for professional growth

| 1 2 3 4 5 6 7 |

	Y N		Y N		Y N		Y N NA
1.1	☐ ☐	3.1	☐ ☐	5.1	☐ ☐	7.1	☐ ☐
1.2	☐ ☐	3.2	☐ ☐	5.2	☐ ☐	7.2	☐ ☐
		3.3	☐ ☐	5.3	☐ ☐	7.3	☐ ☐ ☐
				5.4	☐ ☐		

A. Total Subscale (Items 38–43) Score __ __   B. Number of items scored __ __   **PARENTS AND STAFF Average Score (A ÷ B)** __.__ __

Total and Average Score

	Total Subscale Score	# of Items Scored	Average Score
Space and Furnishings	_____	_____	_____
Personal Care	_____	_____	_____
Language-Reasoning	_____	_____	_____
Activities	_____	_____	_____
Interaction	_____	_____	_____
Program Structure	_____	_____	_____
Parents and Staff	_____	_____	_____
TOTAL	_____	_____	_____

Schedule

Planned   Observed

Substantial Portion of the Day Calculations

Time center opens: __ __ : __ __ ☐AM ☐PM

Time center closes: __ __ : __ __ ☐AM ☐PM

Total hours of operation = ____ hrs ____ mins

Substantial
  portion of the day = ____ hrs ____ mins

REFERENCE CHART

hours	s. portion	hours	s. portion
4	1:20	8	2:40
4½	1:30	8½	2:50
5	1:40	9	3:00
5½	1:50	9½	3:10
6	2:00	10	3:20
6½	2:10	10½	3:30
7	2:20	11	3:40
7½	2:30	11½	3:50
		12	4:00

3. Furnishings for relaxation and comfort Total time = _____ hrs _____ mins	24. Dramatic play Total time = _____ hrs _____ mins
5. Space for privacy Total time = _____ hrs _____ mins	25. Nature/science Total time = _____ hrs _____ mins
15. Books and pictures Total time = _____ hrs _____ mins	26. Math/number Total time = _____ hrs _____ mins
19. Fine motor Total time = _____ hrs _____ mins	34. Schedule Total time = _____ hrs _____ mins
20. Art Total time = _____ hrs _____ mins	35. Free play Total time = _____ hrs _____ mins
22. Block area Total time = _____ hrs _____ mins	

ECERS-R Profile

I. Space & Furnishings (1–8)

Obs. 1 □ Obs. 2 □ average subscale score

1. Indoor space
2. Furn. for routine care, play & learning
3. Furn. for relaxation
4. Room arrangment for play
5. Space for privacy
6. Child-related display
7. Space for gross motor
8. Gross motor equipment

II. Personal Care Routines (9–14)

□

9. Greeting/departing
10. Meals/snacks
11. Nap/rest
12. Toileting/diapering
13. Health practices
14. Safety practices

III. Language-Reasoning (15–18)

□

15. Books and pictures
16. Encouraging children to communicate
17. Using language to develop reasoning skills
18. Informal use of language

IV. Activities (19–28)

□ □

19. Fine motor
20. Art
21. Music/movement
22. Blocks
23. Sand/water
24. Dramatic play
25. Nature/science
26. Math/number
27. Use of TV, video, and/or computers
28. Promoting acceptance of diversity

V. Interaction (29–33)

□ □

29. Supervision of gross motor activities
30. General supervision of children
31. Discipline
32. Staff-child interactions
33. Interactions among children

VI. Program Structure (34–37)

□

34. Schedule
35. Free play
36. Group time
37. Provisions for children with disabilities

VII. Parents and Staff (38–43)

□ □

38. Provisions for parents
39. Provisions for personal needs of staff
40. Provisions for professional needs of staff
41. Staff interaction and cooperation
42. Supervision and evaluation of staff
43. Opportunities for professional growth

Average Subscale Scores

SPACE & FURNISHINGS
PERSONAL CARE
LANGUAGE-REASONING
ACTIVITIES
INTERACTION
PROGRAM STRUCTURE
PARENTS & STAFF

NOTES

NOTES